SCIENCE RESOURCES

Developed at
Lawrence Hall of Science
University of California at Berkeley

Published and Distributed by **Delta Education**

542-0055
ISBN-10: 1-59242-996-3   ISBN-13: 978-1-59242-996-7
3 4 5 6 7 8 9 QWE 12 11 10 09 08 07

The FOSS year 2007 California Edition reflects significant contributions of dedicated professionals in the classroom, their students, administrators, parents, and concerned members of the scientific community. We acknowledge the thousands of educators who have given life to the ideas embodied in the FOSS program. We acknowledge and thank them all for their contributions to the development and implementation of FOSS.

FOSS Grades K–5 California Edition © 2007 Lawrence Hall of Science Team

Larry Malone and Linda De Lucchi, FOSS Project Codirectors and Lead Developers; Kathy Long, Assessment Coordinator; Teri Dannenberg, Developer; Susan Kaschner Jagoda, Developer; Ann Moriarty, Developer; Kimi Hosoume, Developer; Deanne Giffin, Early Childhood Consultant; Joanna Totino, EL Consultant and Professional Developer; Virginia Kammer, EL Consultant; Jaine Kopp and Jenny Maguire, Mathematics Consultants; David Lippman, Editor and Program Specialist; Carol Sevilla, Publications Design Coordinator; Rose Craig, Illustrator; Susan Stanley and Carol Bevilacqua, Graphic Production; Susan Ketchner, Multimedia Director; Alana Chan, FOSSweb Producer; Leigh Anne McConnaughey, Multimedia Artist and Designer; Dan Bluestein, Programmer; Roger Vang, Programmer; John Quick, Photographer; Alev Burton, Administrative Assistant.

FOSS Grades K–5 California Edition © 2007 Delta Education Team

Bonnie Piotrowski, FOSS Editorial Director

Project Team: Lynne Bleeker, Tom Guetling, Joann Hoy, Lisa Lachance, Elizabeth Luzadre, Paulette Miley, Cathrine Monson, Cyndy Patrick, John Prescott, Gary Standafer, Heidi Tyson, Nina Whitney

FOSS Grades K–5 California Edition © 2007 Content Reviewers

David M. Andrews, Ed.D., Professor of Biology and Science Education and Executive Director Science and Mathematics Education Center, California State University, Fresno, CA

Carol Balfe, Ph.D., Science Education Center, California State University of Fresno, CA

Ellen P. Metzger, Ph.D., Professor of Geology, San Jose State University, San Jose, CA

FOSS Grades K–5 California Edition © 2007 Teacher Reviewers

Amy Edmindson, Centralia School, Anaheim, CA; Amy Hellewell, Bonita Canyon School, Irvine, CA; Bonney Waters, Two Bunch Palms Elementary, Desert Hot Springs, CA; Christina Lambie, Highland Elementary, Richmond, CA; Debby Palmer, Turtle Rock Elementary, Irvine, CA; Heinrich Sartin, District 2 Office, North Hollywood, CA; Jeff Self, Washington Elementary, Eureka, CA; Jennifer Faulhaber, G.H. Dysinger School, Buena Park, CA; Jill Garmon, Brywood Elementary, Irvine, CA; Don McKenney, Oakland Unified School District, Oakland, CA; Jill Miles, Sheridan School, Sheridan, CA; Jim Jones, Valley View School, Coachella, CA; Joy Peoples, Riverside School, Riverside, CA; Katherine Jacobs, Verde School, Irvine, CA; Kathy Albrecht, Heritage Oak School, Roseville, CA; Lauren Vu-Tran, Fountain Valley School, Fountain Valley, CA; Lillian Valadez-Rodela, San Pedro MST, San Pedro, CA; Lori Van-Gorp, Anaheim Hills Elementary, Anaheim, CA; Maura Crossin, Local District 4, Los Angeles, CA; Melissa Tallman, College Park Elementary, Irvine, CA; Nancy Lester, Newport Elementary, Newport Beach, CA; Pamela Rockwell, Anaheim Hills Elementary, Anaheim, CA; Rhonda Lemon, Danbrook School, Anaheim, CA; Sherri Ferguson, Brywood Elementary, Irvine, CA; Susan Liberati, Beverly Hills School District, Beverly Hills, CA; Will Neddersen, Tustin USD, Tustin, CA

Production for California © 2007 and © 2003 Editions

LaurelTech Integrated Publishing Services

FOSS 1993–2003 Edition Staff and Contributors

Professor Lawrence F. Lowery, Principal Investigator; Linda De Lucchi, Codirector; Larry Malone, Codirector; Kathy Long, Assessment Coordinator; Leigh Agler, Developer; Susan Kaschner Jagoda, Developer; Kari Rees, Reading Consultant; Carol Sevilla, Graphic Designer; Rose Craig, Illustrator

Contributors: Sara Armstrong, John Quick, Eileen Massey, Joanna Totino, Denise Soderlund, Laura Loutit, Eric Crane, Yiyu Xie, Marco Molinaro, Susan Ketchner, Joannan Gladden, Lisa Haderlie-Baker, Sandra Ragan, Cheryl Webb, Alev Burton, Mark Warren, Marshall Montgomery

FOSS © 2000–2003 Delta Education Team

Mathew Bacon, Grant Gardner, Tom Guetling, Joann Hoy, Dana Koch, Lisa Lachance, Cathrine Monson, Kerri O'Donnell, Bonnie Piotrowski, John Prescott, Jeanette Wall

FOSS Grades K–6 Revision © 2000-2003 Teacher Associates
Claire Kelley, Dennett Elementary School, Plympton, MA
Dyan Van Bishler, Clyde Hill Elementary, Bellevue, WA
Sig Doran, Clyde Hill Elementary, Bellevue, WA
Ann Kumata, John Muir Elementary, Seattle, WA
Kate Shonk, Pleasant Valley Primary, Vancouver, WA
Theresa Fowler, John Rogers Elementary, Seattle, WA
Andrea Edwards, Woodland Primary School, Woodland, WA
Deanne Giffin and Janet Gay, Bancroft Elementary School, Walnut Creek, CA
Jill Kraus, Hawthorne Elementary School, Oakland, CA
Brenda Redmond, Los Perales School, Moraga, CA
Catherine Behymer, Napa Valley Language Academy, Napa, CA
Alison McSweeney, Dennett Elementary, Plympton, MA
Helen Howard and Carol Strandberg, Mt. Erie Elementary, Anacortes, WA
Rondi Peth, Dawn Mayer, and Jeannette Beatty, Fidalgo Elementary, Anacortes, WA
Virginia Kammer, Fresno Unified School District, Fresno, CA
Henrietta Griffitts and Jackie Meylan Dodge, Mt. Diablo Unified School District

Production for © 2000 Edition *FOSS Science Stories*
Creative Media Applications, Inc.
Rhea Baehr, Writer; Michael Burgan, Writer; Robin Doak, Writer; Matthew Dylan, Writer; Emily Lauren, Writer; Matt Levine, Editor; Joanne Mattern, Writer; Dona Smith, Writer; Fabia Wargin, Graphic Design

Original FOSS © 1993–1995 Grades K–6 School District Partners
Kathy Jacobsen, Mt. Diablo Unified School District
Judy Guilkey-Amado and Alexa Hauser, Vallejo City Unified School District
Richard Merrill, Mt. Diablo Unified School District

Original FOSS © 1993–1995 Grades K–6 National Trials Center Directors and Advisers
Directors:
Ramona Anshutz, Kansas State Dept. of Education; Ron Bonnstetter, University of Nebraska; John Cairns, Delaware Dept. of Public Instruction; Arthur Camins, CSD #16, Brooklyn, NY; Winston Hoskins, Garland Independent School District, TX; Rhoda Immer, Siskiyou, County Office of Education, CA; Mildred Jones, New York City Schools; Floyd Mattheis, East Carolina University, NC; Alan McCormack, San Diego State University; Don McCurdy, University of Nebraska; Joseph Premo, Minneapolis Schools; John Staver, Kansas State University, Manhattan, KS; Brian Swagerty, Siskiyou County Office of Education, CA; Sandra Wolford, Colonial School District, New Castle, DE

Advisers:
Sara Armstrong, Heidi Bachman, Carl Berger, Donna Dailey, Robert Dean, Steve Essig, Rosella Jackson, Marsha Knudsen, Catherine Koshland, Samuel Markowitz, Glenn McGlathery, Margaret McIntyre, Shirley McKinney, Richard Merrill, Marshall Montgomery, Gary Nakagiri, Karen Ostlund, John Schippers, Dave Stronck, Dean Taylor, Judy Van Hoorn

FOSS © 1993–1995 Grades K–6 National Trials Leadership Partners
David Allard, Hal Benham, Diane Benham, Arthur Camins, Vicki Clark, John Clementson, Cathy Klinesteker, Karen Dawkins, Sally Dudley, Sheila Dunston, Steve Essig, Fred Fifer, Theresa Flaningam, Chris Foster, Robert Grossman, Cynthia Ledbetter, Charlotte McDonald, Karen Ostlund, Janet Posen, Carlton Robardey, Twyla Sherman, Gerald Skoog, Dean Taylor, Mary Zapata

Published and Distributed by Delta Education, Nashua, NH 03063
The FOSS program was developed in part with the support of the National Science Foundation grants nos. MDR-8751727 and MDR-9150097. However, any opinions, findings, conclusions, statements, and recommendations expressed herein are those of the authors and do not necessarily reflect the views of NSF.

Science Content Standards for California Public Schools reproduced with permission, California Department of Education, CDE Press, 1430 N Street, Suite 3207, Sacramento, CA 95814.

Physical Sciences
Table of Contents

Magnetism and Electricity

Life Sciences
Table of Contents

Environments

Earth Sciences
Table of Contents

Solid Earth

Table of Contents

References

Magnetism and Electricity

Physical Sciences
Table of Contents

Magnetism and Electricity

PS1f. Students know that magnets have two poles (north and south) and that like poles repel each other while unlike poles attract each other.

When Magnet Meets Magnet

You know what a refrigerator **magnet** is. It's an object that might look like a flower, a piece of fruit, or a seashell. And, most importantly, it sticks to the refrigerator.

Refrigerator magnets come in thousands of sizes, colors, and shapes. But, they all have one thing in common. When you look on the back, you see a hard, black object. The hard, black object that sticks to the refrigerator is a **permanent magnet.**

Refrigerator magnets

The magnet may look different from the doughnut-shaped one you used in class. But it works just the same. The pretty picture on the front is just along for the ride.

The most interesting thing about magnets is that they stick to refrigerators and to a lot of other things. But they don't stick to everything. If you test all the different objects around your kitchen, you will soon discover that magnets only stick to some metal things.

A permanent magnet on the back side of a refrigerator magnet

3

After more testing, you will find out that magnets stick to one kind of metal. That metal is **iron.** Iron can be mixed with other metals to make steel. Magnets stick to steel because steel is mostly iron. Magnets do not stick to objects made out of other metals. For example, magnets do not stick to aluminum pots, copper coins, silver spoons, gold rings, or brass hinges. The general rule is, if a magnet sticks to an object, the object is iron or steel.

When two magnets are brought together, the fun begins. Two things can happen. Sometimes magnets pull on each other and actually stick together. When they pull and stick, we say they **attract.**

Two magnets attracting

At other times, magnets push each other apart. When they push apart, we say they **repel.** Why is that?

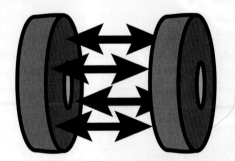

Two magnets repelling

Every magnet has two different sides or ends called **poles.** One pole is called the **south pole,** and the other is called the **north pole.** A simple bar magnet has its two poles on opposite ends. A horseshoe magnet has a pole on each end of the horseshoe. The doughnut magnets you worked with have poles on the two flat sides. Magnets always have a north pole and a south pole.

Bar magnet   Horseshoe magnet   Doughnut magnet

You might wonder what happens when a bar magnet is broken or cut in half. Do you have a magnet with just one pole? No, both pieces still have a north pole and a south pole. The same is true for all other magnets. No matter how many pieces you break a magnet into, each piece still has a north pole and a south pole.

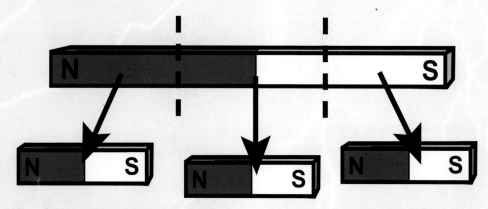

One long bar magnet can be broken into three pieces. Each piece has a north pole and a south pole.

What happens when two magnets come close to each other, and you can feel them repel or push? How are the poles **oriented** or positioned? Do the magnets repel when two south poles come together? Do the magnets repel when two north poles come together? Or do they repel when one south pole and one north pole come together?

Here are four pairs of bar magnets being held together. Which ones will push apart when they are released?

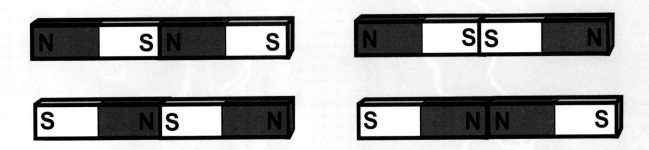

This is what happens when the magnets are released. The two pairs of magnets on the left attract each other. The two pairs of magnets on the right repel each other.

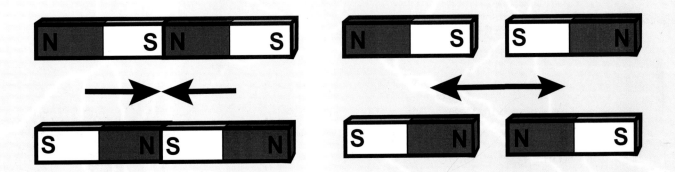

Two south poles always repel each other. Two north poles always repel each other. We can state a general rule. **Like poles repel.**

A south pole and a north pole always attract each other. It doesn't matter which magnet has the south pole and which has the north pole. We can state a second general rule. **Opposite poles attract.**

The Magnetic Force

Magnetism is a **force.** A force is a push or a pull. You can feel the magnetic force when you pull two attracting magnets apart. In the same way, you can feel the magnetic force when you push two repelling magnets together. The force of magnetism is what makes magnets act the ways they do.

How Magnets Stick to Iron

If opposite poles attract, how does a magnet stick to a piece of iron? It's a little mysterious. When a magnet comes close to a piece of iron, the force of magnetism **interacts** with the iron. The iron becomes a **temporary magnet.** The surface of the iron becomes one pole of a magnet. The magnet then sticks to the temporary magnet. So magnets don't really stick to iron. Magnets stick only to other magnets.

The magnetism in the iron is called **induced magnetism.** Induced magnetism happens only when a magnet is close by. If you bring the south pole of a magnet close to a piece of iron, what pole will the surface of the iron become? Just apply the rule. Opposites attract.

The First Magnets

The first magnets were pieces of a naturally occurring magnetic mineral called **magnetite.** All magnetite sticks to magnets because it contains a lot of iron. The black rock in your set of test objects is magnetite. When magnetite is magnetic by itself, it is called **lodestone.**

Lodestone was found in Magnesia.

Legend has it that shepherds found bits of rock sticking to the iron nails in their sandals more than 2,000 years ago. One area rich with lodestone was a part of present-day Turkey. This region was called Magnesia. The word magnet may come from this ancient source of lodestone.

Magnetite is also found in the United States. Can you find the magnetite source closest to California?

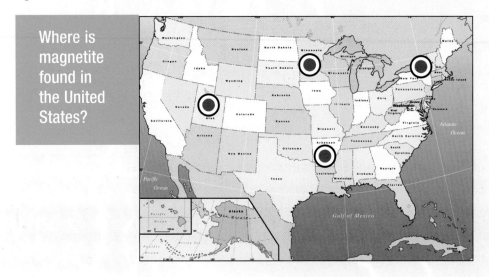

Where is magnetite found in the United States?

Review Questions

1. **What is the most common metal that magnets stick to?**

2. **What causes magnets to attract (stick to) the refrigerator?**

3. **What causes magnets to attract each other at times and repel each other at other times?**

4. **Why does the mineral magnetite stick to a magnet?**

5. **The magnets shown below have one pole labeled. Which pairs of magnets will attract and which will repel?**

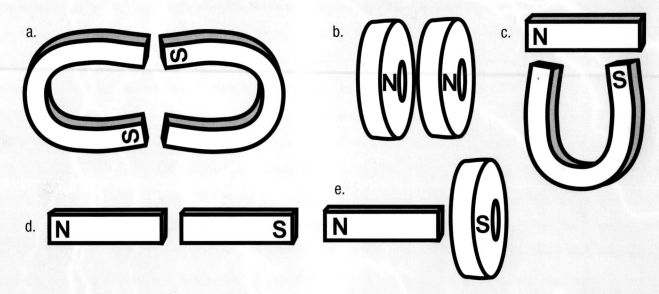

PS1f. Students know that magnets have two poles (north and south) and that like poles repel each other while unlike poles attract each other.

Magnificent Magnetic Models

The ancient Egyptians and Romans used magnets to create artwork! They did not understand magnetic force. But they knew how to do wonderful things with magnets. The Egyptians hung iron and lodestone figures from ropes. The figures would repel and attract each other so that they appeared to dance.

The Romans used magnets to suspend a figure of the god Mercury in midair in one of their temples. You can make models of these statues. Turn the page for the plans.

Egyptian and Roman artwork using magnets

DANCING STATUES

What You Need

2 Plastic film canisters
14 Doughnut magnets
1 Ruler
• String
• Scissors

What You Do

1. Place seven doughnut magnets inside each film canister.
2. Use the scissors to cut a slit in the top of each film canister, from side to center.
3. Slide the string through the slits and tie knots to hold the string in place.
4. Put the tops on the canisters.
5. Hang the string from the ruler.
6. You may have to flip the magnets in one canister over if the two canisters do not repel each other.

What Happens

The canisters dance around each other and never touch.

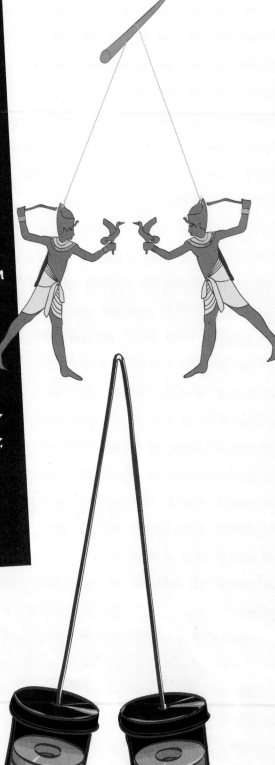

THE SUSPENDED STATUE

What You Need

1   Glass jar with a steel screw-on lid
1   Steel paper clip
1   Magnet
•   Tape
•   Thread

What You Do

1. Stick the magnet to the underside of the jar lid.

2. Tie the paper clip to one end of the thread.

3. Be sure the thread is the right length. The paper clip should almost reach the lid when the thread is taped to the bottom of the jar.

4. Tape the other end of the thread to the bottom of the jar.

5. Hold the jar upside down. Screw on the lid. Then turn the jar upright again. The paper clip should not touch the magnet.

What Happens

The paper clip floats mysteriously at the end of the thread.

Review Questions

1. Explain why the canisters filled with magnets act the way they do.

2. Why doesn't the paper clip fall to the bottom of the jar?

3. Say you wanted to have three canisters of magnets dance around one another. How would you orient the magnets?

INVESTIGATION 1

PS1b. Students know how to build a simple compass and use it to detect magnetic effects, including Earth's magnetic field.

Make a Magnetic Compass

You can make a **compass** just like the one a hiker might use to keep from getting lost. Here's how to do it.

What You Need

1   Bar magnet
1   Ruler
1   Piece of thread about 30 centimeters long (12 inches)
1   Store-bought compass
•   Masking tape

A compass made with a bar magnet, a ruler, and a piece of thread

What You Do

1. Tie one end of the thread to the middle of the magnet so the magnet hangs level.

2. Tie the other end of the thread to the end of the ruler.

3. Tape the ruler at the edge of a table so the magnet hangs in midair. Make sure the magnet is not close to any steel. (Do you know why?) Your compass is done!

When the magnet comes to rest, it will point north and south because it is a compass. But which end points north? You will need a store-bought compass to find out.

The painted end of the store-bought compass needle will point north. Now you should be able to figure out which end of your bar magnet is pointing north.

You can make sure by slowly bringing the store-bought compass up to one end of your hanging bar magnet. Do the compass needle and the magnet point in the same direction? If the answer is yes, then both magnets are pointing north.

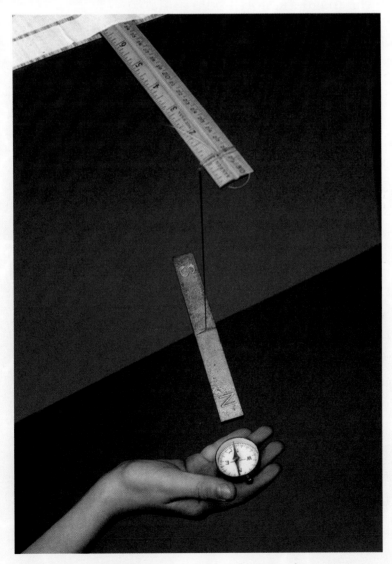

A store-bought compass next to a homemade compass

13

Every magnet has a **magnetic field** around it. Think of a magnetic field as a lot of invisible lines that loop from the north pole to the south pole of a magnet, and then through the magnet. When two magnets interact, it is actually the magnetic fields of the two magnets that interact.

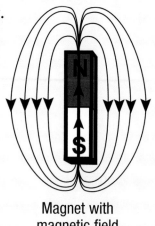

Magnet with magnetic field

Earth is a giant magnet. Magnets all over the planet line up with Earth's magnetic field. The north pole of every free-rotating magnet points to the magnetic north pole of Earth.

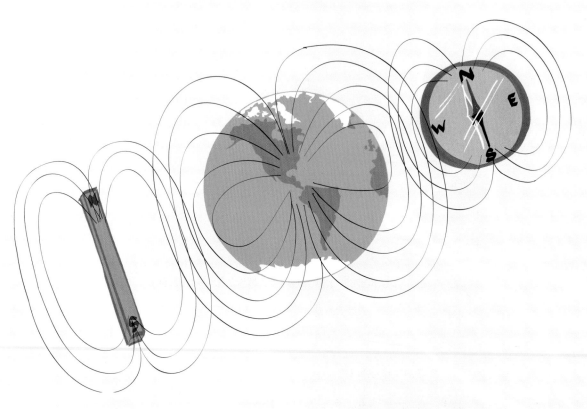

Earth is a giant magnet with a force field around it.

Another Homemade Compass

Make a sewing needle into a permanent magnet by rubbing the needle several times in one direction with a permanent magnet. The needle will have two poles, just like every other permanent magnet.

Push the needle through a piece of plastic foam or cork to make the needle float. When the needle floats in a cup of water, it can rotate to line up with Earth's magnetic field. The needle is a compass!

It's important to keep the needle from drifting over to the side of the water cup. You can use a paper clip to anchor the float. The float and needle can still rotate, and the needle will not get stuck on the side of the cup.

A simple compass made with a steel sewing needle

Review Questions

1. **What is a compass?**

2. **How can you make a compass?**

3. **How do you explain that the north pole of a magnet points toward Earth's North Pole?**

Summary: The Force

Magnets are objects that stick to iron and steel. Magnets are attracted to iron and steel. When a **permanent magnet** gets close to a steel chair leg or door hinge, you can feel a pull between the magnet and the steel. The pull is due to the magnetic **force.**

When two magnets interact, one of two things can happen. The two magnets might **attract** each other and stick together. Or they might **repel** each other and push apart. The things that cause them to attract or repel are the poles on the two magnets.

Every magnet has two poles, a **north pole** and a **south pole.** If the poles approaching each other are the same, the magnets will repel. Two north poles or two south poles will repel each other.

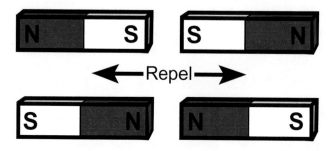

If a north pole approaches a south pole, the magnets will attract.

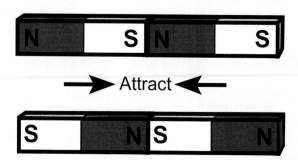

Magnets are surrounded by a **magnetic field.** The field can be thought of as a lot of invisible lines. These lines loop from the north pole to the south pole of a magnet, and then through the magnet.

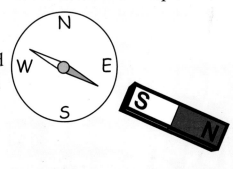

Any piece of iron that enters the magnetic field of a magnet is affected by the field. Iron changes into a temporary magnet. This happens by **induced magnetism.** Magnets that enter the magnetic field of another magnet reorient to line up with the invisible field.

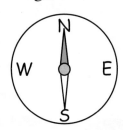

A **compass** is a magnetic needle that is free to rotate at its center. You can make a compass by hanging a magnet on a string. Your compass will respond to the magnetic field of any magnet that is nearby. The north pole of the compass will point to the south pole of an approaching magnet.

Earth is a huge magnet. Because Earth has a magnetic field surrounding it, a compass needle will point toward Earth's magnetic north pole. That's why a compass is a good tool for keeping track of the direction you are hiking.

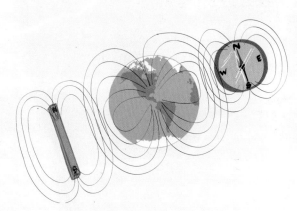

But what might happen if you were hiking in Turkey near old Magnesia? Would your compass work? Maybe not. It might point toward a nearby mound of black **magnetite.** Even a magnetic compass has its limits.

Summary Questions

Now is a good time to review what you have recorded in your science notebook. Think about the investigations you have conducted with magnets.

1. If two magnets are attracting each other, what do you know about the poles?

2. How does a compass work?

3. What will happen if you bring two compasses next to each other?

4. If you have an unmarked bar magnet, how can you find out which end is the north pole?

5. How can you turn a piece of iron into a temporary magnet?

California Science Standards

PS1b. Students know how to build a simple compass and use it to detect magnetic effects, including Earth's magnetic field.

PS1f. Students know that magnets have two poles (north and south) and that like poles repel each other while unlike poles attract each other.

Vocabulary

magnet

permanent magnet

force

attract

repel

north pole

south pole

magnetic field

induced magnetism

compass

magnetite

Extensions

Math Problem of the Week

A teacher wanted to buy some science supplies for her class. She wanted to set up a center in her room where students could explore magnets. She looked in a catalog and found these prices.

Large bar magnets	Set of 2	$10.95
Small bar magnets	Each	$2.75
Large horseshoe magnets	Each	$7.95
Small horseshoe magnets	Each	$4.50
Doughnut magnets	Set of 4	$4.50
Lodestones	Set of 10	$7.95

She has $50.00 to spend. What materials can she buy for the science center? Remember, she can spend only $50.00, and she wants to have different kinds of magnets. Write a short paragraph about why you chose the items you did.

Home/School Connection

Magnets at Home

Find out how magnets are used in your home. Start by finding out what keeps your refrigerator door shut. Talk with your family and then use your imagination to invent something new that uses magnets. Draw a picture of your invention to share with the class. Write a short paragraph that explains what your invention does.

PS1e. Students know electrically charged objects attract or repel each other.

Making Static

Did you ever reach for a doorknob and get a shock? Zap! Why does that happen? Because of **static electricity.**

Static electricity starts with atoms. Atoms are the small particles that everything is made of. Atoms have a nucleus in the center. The nucleus has **positive charge.** Atoms also have tiny **electrons** moving around the nucleus. Electrons have **negative charge.**

Most of the time, the number of positive charges in the nucleus is the same as the number of negative charges moving around the nucleus. When the positive and negative charges are equal, the atom is **electrically neutral.**

Electron Transfer

Sometimes an electron can leave one atom and move to another atom. When this happens, one atom has gained an electron and one has lost an electron. The atom that has gained an electron has negative charge. The atom that lost an electron has positive charge.

Rubbing two objects together can cause electrons to move or **transfer.** When a wool sweater is rubbed on a balloon, electrons transfer from the wool to the rubber. This transfer is how objects can get a static charge.

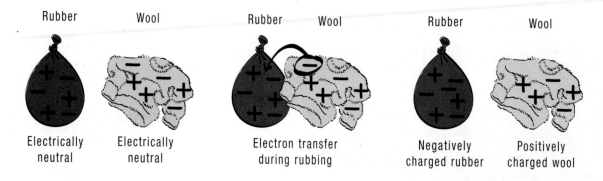

Rubber	Wool	Rubber	Wool	Rubber	Wool
Electrically neutral	Electrically neutral	Electron transfer during rubbing		Negatively charged rubber	Positively charged wool

The Balloon Experiment

When two balloons hang from threads, they come to rest touching each other. The balloons are electrically neutral.

When both balloons are rubbed on a wool sweater or someone's hair, the balloons push each other apart. Why?

During rubbing, electrons transfer from the sweater to the balloons. Both balloons get a negative charge. Negative charges repel each other. That's why the balloons don't touch.

Do you think there is a charge on the wool sweater after rubbing the balloons? If so, is it a negative or positive charge? Remember, electrons transferred from the sweater to the balloons give the balloons a negative charge. That means the sweater lost electrons. The sweater has a positive charge.

What will happen when you bring the positively charged sweater close to the negatively charged balloons? The sweater will attract the balloons. The charge on the wool sweater is opposite to the charge on the balloons. Opposite charges attract.

Two balloons hang side by side when they are electrically neutral.

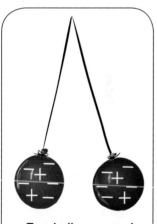

Two balloons repel each other when they have a similar static charge.

Review Questions

1. **Say you wear rubber-soled shoes and walk across a wool rug. What will happen when you reach toward a charged balloon hanging on a string? Why do you think so?**

2. **Say you wear wool slippers and walk across a rubber floor. What will happen when you reach toward a charged balloon hanging on a string? Why do you think so?**

PS1a. Students know how to design and build simple series and parallel circuits by using components such as wires, batteries, and bulbs.

PS1g. Students know electrical energy can be converted to heat, light, and motion.

Edison Sees the Light

Edison with his lightbulb

"The filament burns out too quickly," Mr. Edison said. "We have to find a better material to make the filament last longer."

Thomas Edison (1847–1931) was the most famous inventor of his time. He invented the phonograph, the motion picture camera, the first copy machine, and hundreds of other things. He is most famous, however, for improving a product he *didn't* invent, the electric **lightbulb.**

The problem with lightbulbs before 1879 was that they burned out too quickly. The **filament** is the part of the lightbulb that actually makes the light. When **current electricity** flows through the filament, the filament gets so hot that it glows and gives off light. The hotter the filament gets, the brighter the light. But the hotter the filament gets, the faster it burns out.

Edison's short-lived lightbulb was a simple device. It was much like a modern bulb. In a modern bulb, the filament is held by two stiff support wires. A clear glass globe surrounds the filament for protection. The glass globe is attached to a metal base. The tricky part is how the filament support wires connect to the metal base.

One filament support wire attaches to the side of the metal base. The other support wire attaches to a small metal button at the bottom of the base. The metal button must not touch the main part of the metal base. This is important. When electricity is delivered to the lightbulb in a **circuit,** the electricity must flow *through* the filament.

When the lightbulb is placed in a bulb holder, electricity can be delivered to the bulb. When the circuit is complete, the **electric current** will flow. The electric current has **energy.** The **electric energy** is **converted** (changed) to **heat energy** and **light energy,** and the lightbulb does its job. This is **energy conversion.**

A lightbulb in a circuit

Edison tackled the filament problem in his usual way, with hard work. He is credited with saying, "Invention is one percent inspiration and ninety-nine percent perspiration." Edison directed his team to try every imaginable material to find the best filament. It is said that they tried and rejected 2,000 materials. Edison needed help.

Help came from Lewis Latimer (1848–1928). Latimer was an experienced draftsman and inventor. He had been working on the filament problem, too. Latimer discovered that a carbon-coated cotton thread made a good filament. He got a patent for the carbon filament. Inventors get patents from the government when they invent something new. When Edison tried the carbon filament in his lab, he agreed that it was the best. Edison bought the patent from Latimer so he could use the carbon filament in his lightbulb.

Lewis Latimer

Edison had to solve one more problem before the lightbulb could be used widely. He knew that things need oxygen to burn. If he could remove the air from the glass globe, there would be no oxygen and the filament would not burn up. He was right. This new lightbulb lasted months instead of days.

Thomas Edison had seen the light. Now it was time to show this new light source to the world. It was New Year's Eve, 1879. Edison's team strung lights from its lab to the train station. A crowd of over 3,000 people came to see what would happen.

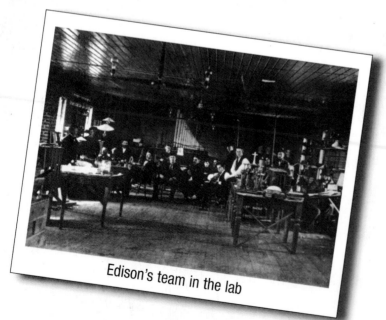
Edison's team in the lab

It was a very dark night, and all the gaslights had been turned off. Edison stepped up to the platform and threw the switch. All the lights came on. The crowd cheered.

Edison understood the importance of electric lighting. It could change the American way of life. That's why he asked Latimer to join his team in 1884. Latimer stayed with Edison for years. He wrote patents for new inventions and books on electrical engineering.

Many years later, in 1918, the team of scientists and engineers gathered to celebrate Edison's birthday. They called themselves the Edison Pioneers. Lewis Latimer was the only African American among the engineers. He also was one of the 28 founding members.

The Edison Pioneers—1920

Review Questions

1. **Edison's lightbulb was an energy converter. What does that mean?**

2. **How does a lightbulb make light?**

3. **Describe the path taken by electricity through a lightbulb.**

Summary: Making Connections

Electrons are the tiny particles that go around the larger nucleus of an atom. Electrons have **negative charge.** The nucleus has **positive charge.** When two materials, such as rubber and wool, are rubbed together, electrons will move from the wool to the rubber. The rubber has more electrons, so it has a negative charge. The wool has fewer electrons, so it has a positive charge.

When two rubber balloons are rubbed on wool, they both get a negative charge. When the two balloons come close to each other, they repel. That's because like charges repel.

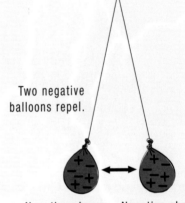

Two negative balloons repel.

Negative charge on rubber   Negative charge on rubber

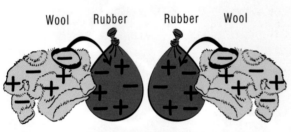

Wool   Rubber   Rubber   Wool

Electron transfer during rubbing

Two objects with a negative charge always repel. Two objects with a positive charge also repel. But if one object with a positive charge comes close to an object with a negative charge, the objects will attract. Opposite charges attract.

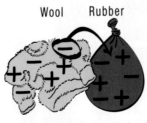

Wool   Rubber

Electron transfer during rubbing

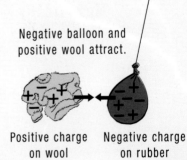

Negative balloon and positive wool attract.

Positive charge on wool   Negative charge on rubber

Current Electricity

Charge on the move is **current electricity.** A D-cell is a source of current electricity. A copper wire is an electricity **conductor.** If a copper wire is connected from one end of the D-cell to the other, current electricity will flow from the negative end of the cell to the positive end of the cell. Electricity flows in a pathway called a **circuit.** A wire from one end of a cell to the other is the simplest circuit.

A short circuit

Making a circuit by connecting the two ends of a D-cell with a wire is not a good thing to do. This creates a **short circuit.** Short circuits drain the energy from D-cells very rapidly. You always want to have something like a lightbulb or a motor in the circuit.

Using Electric Energy

Electricity is a form of **energy. Electric energy** can be used to do work. By putting different lightbulbs or motors in circuits with an electricity source, we can turn electric energy into other kinds of energy. This is called **energy conversion.**

Conversion means change. When a lightbulb is put in a circuit with a D-cell, the electric energy is converted into **light energy.** When a motor is put in a circuit with a D-cell, the shaft turns. The electric energy is converted into **motion energy.** When you plug in a fan, electric energy is converted to motion energy. At home when you plug a toaster into the wall socket, electric energy is converted into **heat energy.**

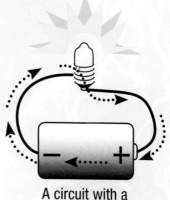

A circuit with a lightbulb

Summary Questions

Now is a good time to review what you have recorded in your science notebook. Think about the investigations you have conducted using electrically charged objects. Think about the circuits you built using D-cells, motors, lightbulbs, switches, and wires.

1. What do you think would happen if you combed your hair with a rubber comb and then brought the comb near a balloon that had been rubbed on wool? Why would that happen?

2. What do you call a pathway through which electricity flows from one end of a cell to the other?

3. Electric lights get hot when they are used. What energy conversions are happening?

4. What are conductors and insulators?

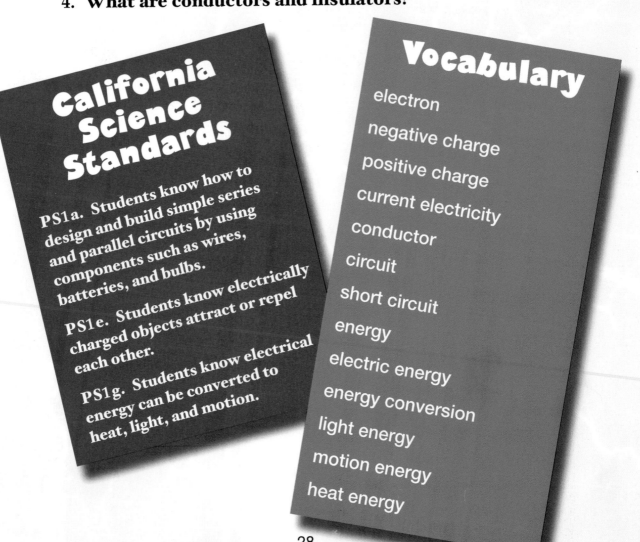

California Science Standards

PS1a. Students know how to design and build simple series and parallel circuits by using components such as wires, batteries, and bulbs.

PS1e. Students know electrically charged objects attract or repel each other.

PS1g. Students know electrical energy can be converted to heat, light, and motion.

Vocabulary

electron

negative charge

positive charge

current electricity

conductor

circuit

short circuit

energy

electric energy

energy conversion

light energy

motion energy

heat energy

Extensions

Math Problem of the Week

A fourth-grade class wanted to find out how many hours different brands of C-cells would last. Students bought three Charger cells, three E-Z Volt cells, and three Amp-Champ cells. They hooked up each cell to a motor, let it run each day while they were in class, and unhooked it at night when they went home. Below is what they observed.

Charger 1	30 hours
Charger 2	25 hours
Charger 3	20 hours
E-Z Volt 1	30 hours
E-Z Volt 2	40 hours
E-Z Volt 3	35 hours
Amp-Champ 1	25 hours
Amp-Champ 2	40 hours
Amp-Champ 3	40 hours

Based on these data, which brand of cells would you buy? Explain why you chose that brand.

Home/School Connection

Where's the Electricity?

Make a list of electric fixtures and appliances in your home. Write some rules and practices for using electricity safely.

Use the Home/School Connection sheet called *Where's the Electricity?* to record the fixtures and appliances. Or make up your own way to organize your list.

PS1a. Students know how to design and build simple series and parallel circuits by using components such as wires, batteries, and bulbs.

Series and Parallel Circuits

Electric energy comes from an electricity source. The source might be a D-cell, battery, or wall socket. When a **component,** like a lightbulb, is connected to a source of electricity, the bulb will make light. When a different component, like a motor, is connected to an electricity source, the motor shaft will turn. How do you connect a lightbulb or a motor to an electricity source?

A D-cell can be used to light a lightbulb. Metal wires can be used to carry the electricity. If you try to get the bulb to shine using one wire like this, the lightbulb will not shine.

An incomplete circuit

The trick is to use two wires. One wire connects the side of the bulb to one end of the D-cell. The second wire connects the base of the bulb to the other end of the D-cell. This setup results in a brightly shining lightbulb. It is called a **complete circuit,** or a **closed circuit.** The places on a D-cell and bulb where wires touch the component are called **contacts.**

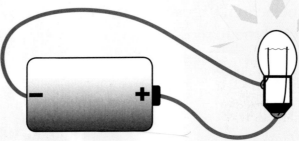

A complete or closed circuit

If one of the wires is disconnected from the lightbulb or from the D-cell, the bulb will stop shining. This is because the pathway through which the electricity flows to the bulb is broken. A circuit with a break is called an **incomplete circuit,** or an **open circuit.**

It is important where the wires connect to the D-cell and the lightbulb. One wire must connect to the positive (+) end of the cell. The other wire must connect to the negative (−) end of the cell. The other end of one of the wires must connect to the side of the lightbulb. The other end of the second wire must connect to the base of the lightbulb. These connections make a closed circuit. The electricity will flow, and the lightbulb will shine.

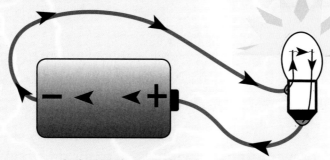

A simple circuit with a D-cell and a lightbulb

You might want to connect two lightbulbs to a D-cell. How can you do this? There are two ways to do it. You can open the one-bulb circuit and put a second bulb into the circuit. Now the electricity flows through two lightbulbs in one circuit. This is a **series circuit.** There are two bulbs and one D-cell connected in series. In a series circuit, there is only one pathway for electricity to flow from the electricity source (D-cell) to the components (lightbulbs).

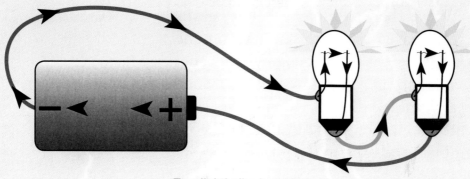

Two lightbulbs in series

There is another way to add a second bulb to the one-bulb circuit. You use two wires to connect the second bulb to the first bulb. This is called a **parallel circuit.** There are two bulbs in parallel connected to a D-cell. In this parallel circuit, each component (lightbulb) has its own pathway to the electricity source (D-cell).

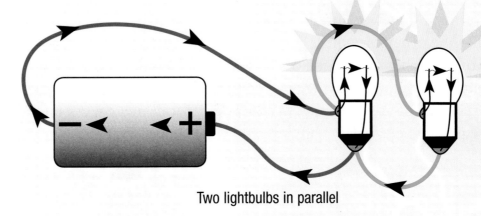

Two lightbulbs in parallel

Which Circuit Should You Use?

Lightbulbs, D-cells, and wires can be represented by symbols. Circuits can be drawn using the symbols. Circuit drawings using symbols are called **schematic diagrams.**

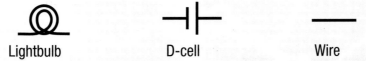

Lightbulb   D-cell   Wire

Say you want to light two bulbs. Is there any reason to put them in series rather than in parallel? Yes. The reason becomes clear when you compare the two kinds of circuits. Two bulbs in series both glow with a dim light. Both bulbs in parallel shine brightly. If you want bright lights, put the bulbs in parallel.

Why is there a difference? Two lightbulbs in series have to share the energy from the D-cell. There is only one pathway for the electric current. The current flows from the negative end of the cell, through the first lightbulb. It then goes through the second lightbulb, and back to the positive end of the cell.

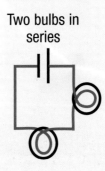

Two bulbs in series

Two lightbulbs in parallel do not have to share energy from the D-cell. Each bulb has its own pathway to the source of electricity. That's why both bulbs shine brightly. In this schematic diagram, the pathway of one bulb is red. The pathway for the other bulb is blue. The two bulbs share one wire for part of their pathways.

Two bulbs in parallel

One wire shared by both bulbs

So, is it better to connect your lightbulbs in series or in parallel? It seems like parallel would be better because you get two bright lights. But there is a cost. The D-cell will drain much faster when it is supplying electricity to two lightbulbs in parallel. When bulbs are connected in series, the D-cell lasts longer, but the lights are dimmer.

Adding More D-cells to a Circuit

If you want to put two or more D-cells in a circuit, they can be connected in series or in parallel. Which of these drawings shows two cells in series? Which shows two cells in parallel?

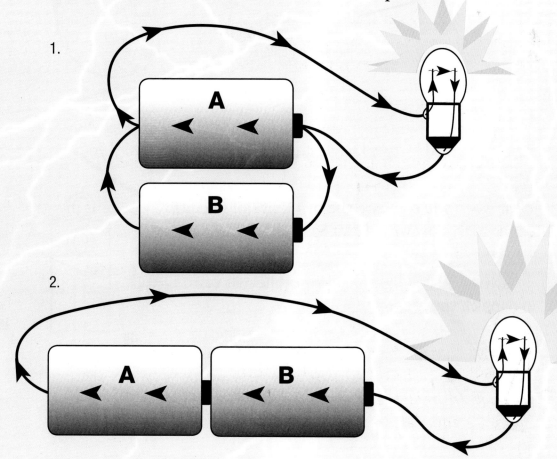

1.

A

B

2.

A   B

In circuit 1, cells A and B are in parallel. Each cell delivers electricity to the lightbulb in its own pathway. In circuit 2, electricity is delivered to the lightbulb by two cells working together in the same pathway. As a result, the lightbulb in circuit 2 will be twice as bright as the bulb in circuit 1.

Here is an interesting circuit made with lightbulbs and D-cells. How would you describe this circuit?

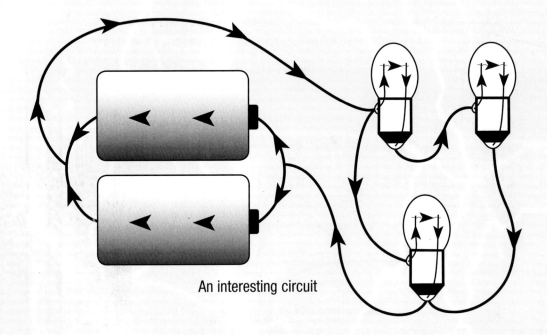

An interesting circuit

This circuit is one lightbulb in parallel with two lightbulbs in series, powered by two D-cells in parallel. If you said that, you got it.

A student made a circuit with two lightbulbs and two D-cells. How would you describe the circuit in this schematic diagram?

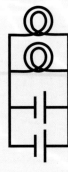

If you said two lightbulbs in parallel with two D-cells in parallel, you are right.

Review Questions

1. **What is the advantage of wiring two lightbulbs in parallel?**

2. **Why are two bulbs in series with a D-cell dim?**

3. **Do you think the lights in your home are wired in series or in parallel? Why do you think so?**

4. **Here are schematic diagrams for eight circuits. How would you describe each circuit? (See the description at the bottom of page 34 as an example.)**

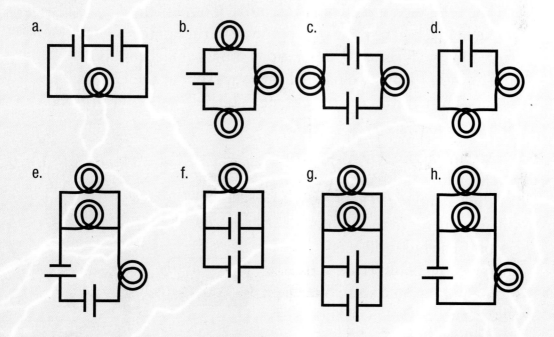

a.   b.   c.   d.

e.   f.   g.   h.

Summary: Advanced Connections

Components can be connected to a source of electricity to make circuits. If you have two components, they can be connected to the source in two different ways. One way is a **series circuit.** This illustration shows a lightbulb and a motor in series.

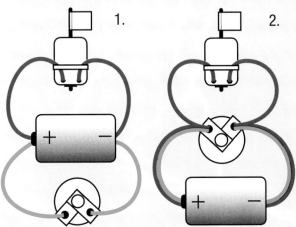

Circuit with D-cell, bulb, and motor

The other way is a **parallel circuit.** Components in parallel each have their own pathway to the source of electricity. These two illustrations show parallel circuits. In illustration 1 the two parallel pathways split at the D-cell. The motor gets energy in the red circuit. The bulb gets energy in the blue circuit.

In illustration 2 the two parallel pathways split at the lightbulb contacts. The motor still gets energy in the red circuit. The bulb still gets energy in the blue circuit. The motor and the bulb share one wire between the D-cell and the bulb.

D-cells can be used in series and parallel with components. When two cells are placed in series with a lightbulb, the bulb might shine brighter than it will with one D-cell. One of the series circuits shown here will make very bright light. The other will not make light at all. Can you see why?

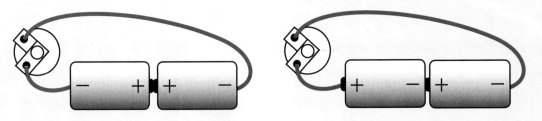

D-cells can also be put in parallel. When two D-cells in parallel are connected to a lightbulb, the bulb will make light only as bright as with one D-cell. But the lightbulb will glow twice as long as it will with one D-cell.

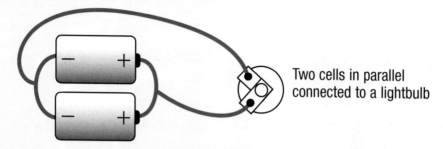

Two cells in parallel connected to a lightbulb

Schematic diagrams are good ways to record circuits. The two cells in parallel connected to a lightbulb above look like this.

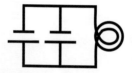

Complex circuits can be explained easily with schematic diagrams. Can you describe the two circuits on this page? Find the right diagrams in the schematics in the summary questions on page 38.

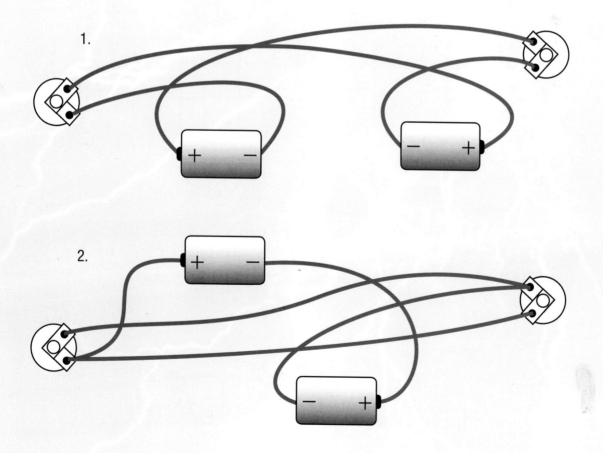

1.

2.

Summary Questions

Now is a good time to review what you have recorded in your science notebook. Think about the investigations you have conducted using series and parallel circuits.

1. **Many flashlights use two D-cells. Are the D-cells used in series or in parallel with the lightbulb? Why?**

2. **Would you recommend wiring strings of lights in series or in parallel? Why?**

3. **Which schematic diagram below represents circuit 1 on page 37?**

4. **How would you describe circuit 1 in words?**

5. **Which schematic diagram below represents circuit 2 on page 37?**

6. **How would you describe circuit 2 in words?**

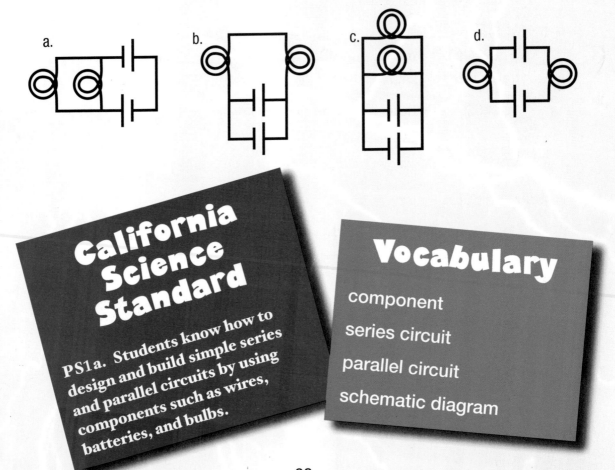

Vocabulary

component

series circuit

parallel circuit

schematic diagram

Extensions

Math Problem of the Week

A student wants to predict how many wires she will need before she starts building circuits. Can you help her find a pattern?

1. What if she builds series circuits with one strong D-cell and some lightbulbs?
2. What if she builds series circuits with one D-cell, a switch, and any number of bulbs?
3. What if she builds series circuits with one D-cell for every bulb she includes?
4. What if she builds a parallel circuit with one D-cell and some lightbulbs?

One way to solve these problems is to look for patterns so you can find the answer no matter how many bulbs are used. You might start with a simple series circuit with one bulb and one D-cell and then build from there.

You should be able to see the pattern. You always need one more wire than bulb (B + 1 = W). So, if you put 100 lights in the circuit, you would need 101 wires.

Use the same method or one of your own to solve questions 2–4.

Home/School Connection

What's Inside an Electric Appliance?

Take a look inside a small broken electric or electronic device, such as a radio, tape player, or remote control. You will see complex circuits.

Use the Home/School Connection sheet called *What's Inside an Electronic Appliance?* to record some of the components you discover.

Safety Note: Ask an adult to remove power cords from plug-in devices before you explore the insides.

PS1c. Students know electric currents produce magnetic fields and know how to build a simple electromagnet.

Electricity = Magnetism

Oersted's Discovery

In 1820 Hans Christian Oersted made a simple observation. He was demonstrating that electric current makes wires hot. When he closed the electric circuit, a compass needle that happened to be on his lab table rotated. Oersted wondered why.

Oersted was born in Denmark in 1777. Young Hans never went to school. His parents sent him to Germany, where he worked in a shop. During those years he learned to read and became skilled with math. When he was 11 years old, Hans returned home and went to work in his father's pharmacy. There he learned the basics of chemistry.

Hans Christian Oersted (1777–1851)

Even without any schooling, Oersted passed the exam to enter the University of Copenhagen, in Denmark. He studied chemistry, astronomy, physics, and math. After he graduated, he became a physics professor at the university.

Like many scientists of his time, Oersted was fascinated with the discovery made by Alessandro Volta in the year 1800. Volta invented the battery, which was the first source of current electricity. The D-cell we use today is a direct result of Volta's discovery. Oersted conducted lots of experiments with current electricity.

Oersted thought that there must be some connection between current electricity and magnetism, but he had no evidence. He was giving a lecture on current electricity and heat when he observed the rotating compass needle. Some people think he was planning to show the relationship between current electricity and magnetism that day in April 1820. Others think it was just a lucky accident. We will never know for sure.

Here's what may have happened. Oersted had a thin wire connected to a battery and a switch. A compass needle happened to be right under one of the wires forming the circuit.

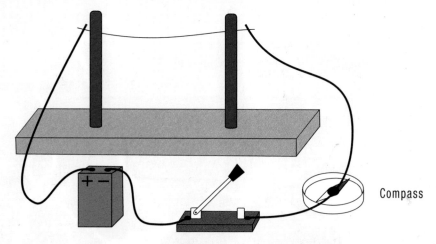

Oersted's demonstration with the switch open

When the circuit was closed to deliver electric current to the thin wire, the compass needle rotated.

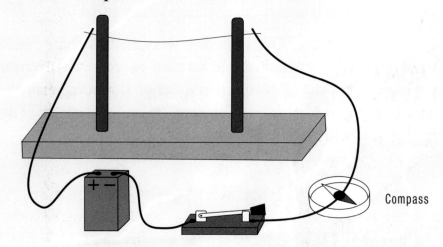

Oersted's demonstration with the switch closed

Oersted must have been excited, but he didn't announce his discovery at that time. He conducted more experiments. Four months later he wrote a report of his finding. His conclusion was that a flow of current electricity produces a magnetic field.

This important discovery resulted in hundreds of inventions in the years that followed. One was the **electromagnet,** a magnet that can be turned on and off.

Magnetic Fields

The magnetic field around a wire with electric current flowing through it is not very strong. If you can put two magnetic fields together, the magnetism will be stronger. That's what happens when a wire is wound into a **coil.** The magnetic field around each coil adds to the fields from other coils. The greater the number of coils, the stronger the total magnetic field.

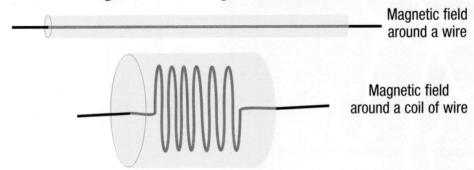

Magnetic field around a wire

Magnetic field around a coil of wire

When the coil is wrapped around an iron or steel **core,** like a rivet, the strong magnetic field induces magnetism in the steel. The steel becomes a magnet as long as the current is flowing. And, with a flip of the switch, the magnetism turns off.

It wasn't long after Oersted's discovery that Michael Faraday discovered that magnetism could be used to create a current of electricity. From that time on, there was no doubting that one force was responsible for both magnetism and electricity. That force is the electromagnetic force.

Review Questions

1. **What was Oersted's historic discovery?**

2. **How does an electromagnet work?**

3. **Why did Oersted's compass needle rotate when he ran electric current through the thin wire?**

PS1c. Students know electric currents produce magnetic fields and know how to build a simple electromagnet.

How Electromagnetism Stopped a War

This is the story of how a famous magician used science to stop a war. It happened almost two centuries ago.

In 1805 a French clock maker and his wife had a son. They named him Jean-Eugène Robert (1805–1871). Jean-Eugène grew up to be a skilled clock maker himself. In 1829 he married the daughter of another skilled clock maker and added her last name to his—Jean-Eugène Robert-Houdin.

Robert-Houdin was fascinated by mechanical things. He made mystery clocks with invisible workings, mechanical singing birds, and a robot. Whenever a new book on clock making came out, he read it. It was, in fact, a clock-making book that changed his life. By accident, a bookseller delivered Robert-Houdin a book about science and magic instead of the book he ordered. It showed how magicians used scientific discoveries to do "magic." He stayed up late into the night reading the book and studying the illustrations. That night, Robert-Houdin became a magician.

Over the next ten years, Robert-Houdin studied and performed magic. He learned to make cards vanish and coins appear from thin air. By day, he made clocks. At night, he made magic.

One of Robert-Houdin's mystery clocks

At age 40, Robert-Houdin became a stage magician. He performed throughout Europe. Robert-Houdin was the most famous magician of his time.

In the mid-1800s France ruled the country of Algeria. The Algerians wanted to break away from French rule. They were ready to go to war with the French.

The French leaders didn't want to go to war. They knew that the Algerians were impressed by magical powers. The French asked Robert-Houdin to help. Maybe he could convince the Algerians that the French had magical powers. Maybe this could stop the war.

Jean-Eugène Robert-Houdin

Robert-Houdin agreed to try. On October 28, 1856, he performed for the Algerian leaders. He used the power of science to create his special magic.

Many years before, Hans Christian Oersted had made an important discovery. A wire conducting electric current produces a magnetic field. When electric current flowed through an insulated wire wrapped around an iron bar, the bar became an electromagnet. When the current stopped, the iron bar lost its magnetism.

Robert-Houdin used his knowledge of electromagnets to design his magic trick. He built a stage over a huge electromagnet. The electromagnet could be turned on and off with a hidden switch. Then he made a wooden chest with an iron bottom. The stage was set.

The Algerian leaders were invited to a meeting with the French. Robert-Houdin challenged one of the leaders to pick up the wooden chest. The man easily lifted it. Then Robert-Houdin shouted, "Behold! I now cast a spell on you. You are now weaker than a child." The man tried to lift the chest again, but he could not move it.

To prove his magic power, Robert-Houdin invited a child to lift the box. To everyone's surprise, the child lifted it. Then Robert-Houdin had the Algerian leader try again. The box would not budge! The audience gasped.

Four days later, Robert-Houdin was invited to the governor's palace. The Algerian leaders wore red robes. This was a symbol of their loyalty to France. The Algerian leaders feared that Robert-Houdin's magic could make their soldiers too weak to fight. Robert-Houdin's magnetic trick stopped the war!

Review Questions

1. **What did Robert-Houdin know about science that helped him outsmart the Algerian leaders?**

2. **How did Robert-Houdin get a wooden chest to stick to his electromagnet?**

3. **What do you think Robert-Houdin did to make his electromagnet so strong?**

Summary:
Current Attractions

The wire you have been using to make circuits is made of copper. Copper wire is not magnetic. There is no magnetic field around a copper wire. You can see this is true by bringing a compass close to a copper wire. The compass needle does not move.

Things change when you connect a copper wire to a source of electricity, such as a D-cell. While **electric current** is flowing through the wire, a **magnetic field** surrounds it. When you bring a compass close to the wire, the compass needle will rotate. When the circuit is broken, the magnetic field disappears, and the compass needle points north again.

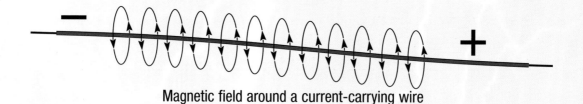

Magnetic field around a current-carrying wire

The fact that a current produces a magnetic field can be used to make a very useful device. This device is an **electromagnet.** An electromagnet is a magnet that can be turned on and off with the flip of a switch.

The magnetic field surrounding a current-carrying wire is not very strong. The strength of the field can be increased by coiling the wire. When two **coils** are next to each other, the magnetic fields add together. This makes the magnetic field stronger.

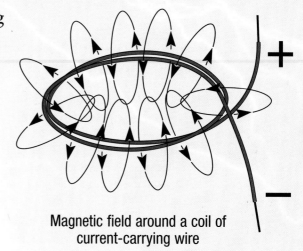

Magnetic field around a coil of current-carrying wire

As you add more coils, the magnetic field gets stronger and stronger. If you put an iron **core,** like a rivet, in the center of the coils, the strong magnetic field will induce magnetism in the iron. That is how electromagnets are made.

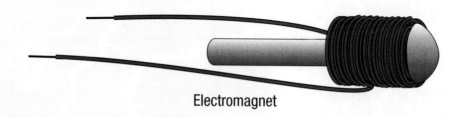

Electromagnet

There are several ways to make an electromagnet stronger. More coils of wire is one way that you have already learned about. The more wire you wrap around the core, the stronger the magnetism.

Another way to make an electromagnet stronger is to increase the amount of electricity flowing through the wire. You used one D-cell. Two D-cells increase the magnetism a lot. What if you had ten D-cells in series? Or 100 D-cells in series? Now we're talking about some strong magnetism.

A third way to make an electromagnet stronger is to wrap thicker wire around the core. Thicker wire can conduct more electricity. The thicker the wire, the stronger the magnetic field, and the stronger the electromagnet.

There are a couple of other things you always need to think about. The wire must be insulated. (Do you know why?) And the coils of wire must all be wound around the core in the same direction. It doesn't matter which direction as long as they all go the *same* direction.

Summary Questions

Now is a good time to review what you have recorded in your science notebook. Think about the investigations you have conducted with electromagnets.

1. **What is one way to tell if a wire has current flowing through it?**

2. **How do you make an electromagnet?**

3. **What are three ways to make an electromagnet stronger?**

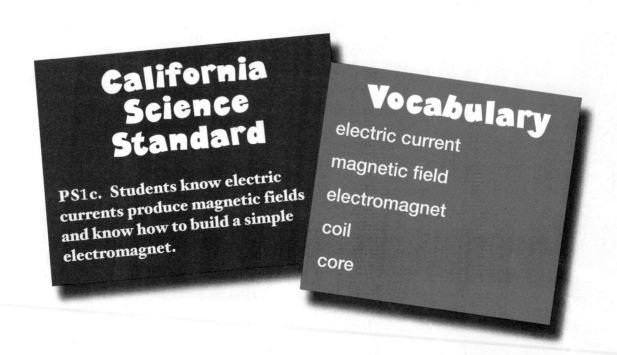

California Science Standard

PS1c. Students know electric currents produce magnetic fields and know how to build a simple electromagnet.

Vocabulary

electric current

magnetic field

electromagnet

coil

core

Extensions

Math Problem of the Week

A class in San Diego just finished the electromagnet investigation. The students want to compare results with their FOSS science pals in Fresno. They want to find out if electromagnets work the same in the two cities. The classes exchange results for electromagnets with 20 winds and with 40 winds. They think it would be best to compare the averages of the results.

Average the results for the classes. Do electromagnets work the same in San Diego as in Fresno? Why or why not?

SAN DIEGO

GROUP	20 WINDS	40 WINDS
1	14 washers	30 washers
2	15 washers	35 washers
3	14 washers	28 washers
4	13 washers	38 washers
5	16 washers	41 washers
6	17 washers	33 washers
7	19 washers	29 washers
8	20 washers	30 washers

FRESNO

GROUP	20 WINDS	40 WINDS
1	18 washers	23 washers
2	13 washers	30 washers
3	16 washers	31 washers
4	17 washers	27 washers
5	20 washers	42 washers
6	18 washers	33 washers

Home/School Connection

Fuses and Circuit Breakers

Read the short paragraph about fuses and circuit breakers on the Home/School Connection sheet called *Fuses and Circuit Breakers*. With an adult, locate the fuse or circuit-breaker box in your home to find out how many circuits there are. Try to find where the main supply line enters the box. Look for how the line splits into several smaller circuits that deliver electricity to different parts of your home. Use the *Fuses and Circuit Breakers* sheet to keep track of your discoveries.

Safety Note: Ask an adult to work with you on this activity.

PS1d. Students know the role of electromagnets in the construction of electric motors, electric generators, and simple devices, such as doorbells and earphones.

Morse Gets Clicking

Samuel F. B. Morse

Imagine what it would be like without the telephone. How would you keep in touch with your friends? That's the way it was 170 years ago. There were no phones, radios, or televisions. There were no computers for e-mail. People wrote letters. It could take weeks or months to receive a letter and respond to it.

In 1820 Hans Christian Oersted discovered that a wire carrying an electric current produced a magnetic field. In 1825 the electromagnet was invented. It was known that electricity moved fast through wires. Could electricity be changed into words to speed up communication?

Samuel F. B. Morse (1791–1872) had an idea how to make electricity "speak." In 1835 Morse used an electromagnet, a switch, and long wires to send a long-distance message. The switch (called a **key**) and a battery were in one location. Long wires ran to an electromagnet far away. When the key was pressed to complete the circuit, the electromagnet attracted a piece of steel with a loud click. Those first clicks announced the birth of the **telegraph.**

Morse knew his telegraph could change the way people communicated. But he had trouble finding others who agreed. Finally, eight years later, he got a $30,000 grant to set up a telegraph line from the railroad station in Baltimore, Maryland, to the Supreme Court building in Washington, DC. The next year, in 1844, the first message traveled the 65 kilometers (40 miles) between the two cities in a fraction of a second. In moments the return message reached Morse. The telegraph was a success.

Morse's telegraph was not very different from the one you made in class. The key was similar to your switch. The batteries were stronger. The electromagnet had more winds of wire to make it stronger.

The electromagnet used by Morse

The key used by Morse

The telegraph you made in class

Putting the Message into Words

There's one more important part to this story. Remember, the telegraph didn't send words, it just sent clicks. How can you make words out of clicks? Morse needed a **code** to translate clicks into words.

The first code Morse tried didn't work very well. The receiver had a pen attached to the electromagnet. When the circuit was closed, the pen moved and made a mark on a roll of paper. The dots and squiggles were too hard to decode.

Next Morse developed a code where clicks stood for words. For instance, one click might be the word *you*. Two rapid clicks might be the word *today*. Two widely spaced clicks might be the word *now,* and so on. The code book was huge. It took a long time to look up the words after a set of clicks was received.

The code that worked was developed by Morse and his partner, Alfred Vail, in 1838. It used short and long sounds, called dots and dashes, to stand for letters of the alphabet. You might wonder how Morse got his telegraph to make short and long clicks. He didn't. The short and long "sounds" were actually the pauses between the clicks. The telegraph receiver heard the short and long pauses between clicks as the dots and dashes.

Here is the present-day Morse code.

A	.-	I	..	R	.-.	1	.----
B	-...	J	.---	S	...	2	..---
C	-.-.	K	-.-	T	-	3	...--
Ch	----	L	.-..	U	..-	4	....-
D	-..	M	--	V	...-	5	.....
E	.	N	-.	W	.--	6	-....
F	..-.	O	---	X	-..-	7	--...
G	--.	P	.--.	Y	-.--	8	---..
H	....	Q	--.-	Z	--..	9	----.
						0	-----

Period	.-.-.-
Comma	--..--
Colon	---...
Question mark	..--..
Apostrophe	.----.
Hyphen	-....-
Slash	-..-.
Right parenthesis	-.--.-
Left parenthesis	-.--.
Quotation marks	.-..-.

What Happened to the Telegraph

After the Baltimore-to-Washington message in 1844, the telegraph became popular. Every major city had a central telegraph office. Businesses and governments depended on the telegraph for the fast delivery of news.

Science was moving forward, however. In Italy, a young engineer named Guglielmo Marconi (1874–1937) was experimenting with a device that sent and received signals right through the air. No wires were needed! Marconi discovered that electric discharges, like strong sparks, sent radiation waves (a kind of energy) in all directions into space. By turning the spark on and off, Marconi could send dots and dashes out into the air.

An antenna could catch the waves and convert them into short and long pulses of electricity. When the pulses of electricity flowed through a wire coil, they created an electromagnet. When the electromagnet was repelled by a permanent magnet, it made sound. The sound came in dots and dashes, exactly as they had been sent by the sparker. The wireless system is called radio.

The first radio messages were sent in 1895. In 1899 radio messages in Morse code were being sent across the English Channel. In 1901 radio signals were sent across the Atlantic Ocean. As radio became more popular, the telegraph was used less and less. By the time commercial radio, with music and voice, appeared in 1920, the telegraph had just about faded from the scene.

Review Questions

1. **How is an electromagnet used in a telegraph?**

2. **How is the telegraph you made like the one Morse made?**

3. **When your telegraph does not have enough power to make a click, you might have to modify your system. Can you decode these suggestions from Morse?**

   .- -.. -.. / -- --- .-. . / -.-. . .-.. .-.. ... -.-

   ..- ... . / -- --- .-. . / -.. --- .. -.. ... -.-

PS1d. Students know the role of electromagnets in the construction of electric motors, electric generators, and simple devices, such as doorbells and earphones.

PS1g. Students know electrical energy can be converted to heat, light, and motion.

Electromagnets Everywhere

Motors

A motor that runs off a D-cell is a direct-current motor. A direct-current motor has two main parts. They are permanent magnets and electromagnets.

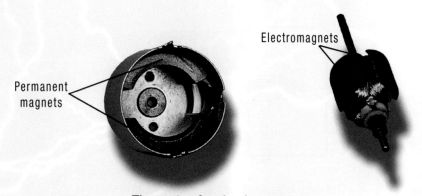

Permanent magnets

Electromagnets

The parts of a simple motor

A simple motor is like a tin can with two permanent magnets stuck inside. In the center of the can, there is a shaft with three iron cores attached. A lot of wire is wrapped around each of the cores to make electromagnets.

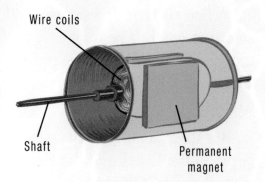

Wire coils

Shaft

Permanent magnet

Imagine taking the permanent magnets and shaft out of the can. Take off all but one of the wire coils. The simplified motor would look like the one below.

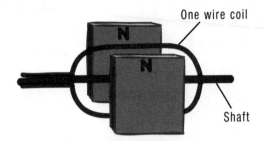

One wire coil

Shaft

A simplified motor with two permanent
magnets and only one wire coil

Connect the wire to a source of electric current, such as a D-cell. The flow of current makes a magnetic field around the wire.

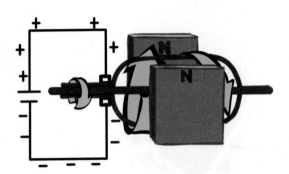

The wire coil becomes an electromagnet when
it is connected to a D-cell.

When current flows in the coil, the coil becomes an electromagnet. The magnetic field of the electromagnet is repelled by the field of the permanent magnet. (Like poles repel.) This pushes the electromagnet away. The push causes the shaft to rotate.

But there is more to the design. When the shaft rotates, contact between the D-cell and the electromagnet is broken. The current stops flowing in the coil. The electromagnetism stops briefly.

As the shaft rotates a little farther, contact is made again. This creates the electromagnetic field in the coil again. The coil gets another magnetic push to keep the shaft turning.

The shaft gets hundreds of little magnetic pushes every second. This **converts** electric energy into motion energy.

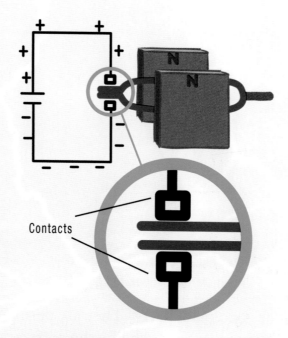

As the shaft rotates, contact between the D-cell and the coil is broken. As the shaft rotates a little farther, contact is made again.

Generators

You know how to use electricity to make a flashlight work. You get some D-cells. But where does the electricity in your house come from? It does not come from batteries. The electricity in your house comes from a **generator.** Generators convert motion into electric energy.

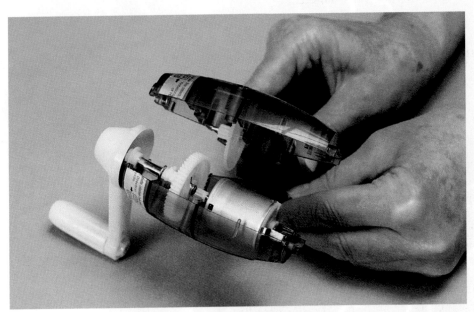

A simple hand-operated generator

A generator has two main parts. They are permanent magnets and wire coils. They are very much like the parts found in a motor. A direct-current generator is a motor running in reverse.

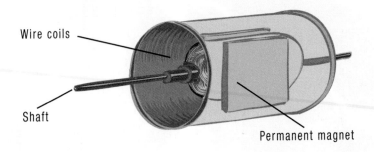

When you put electricity into a motor, you get motion. When you rotate the shaft of the motor, you get electricity. It's amazing but true. Here's how it works.

There is a magnetic field between the poles of the permanent magnets. A shaft with wire coils is placed between the magnets. Take off all but one of the wire coils. The simplified generator would look like the diagram on the right.

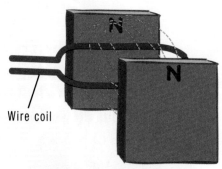

When a wire coil turns in a magnetic field, an electric current is created in the wire.

When a wire passes through a magnetic field, an electric current is created in the wire. If you rotate a wire coil in a magnetic field, it will pass through the field hundreds of times in a second. This makes a continuous flow of current electricity.

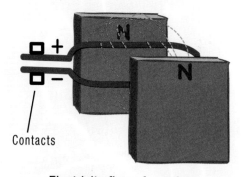

Electricity flows from the generator when contact is made with the end of the wire coil.

What turns the wire coil in the magnetic field? The answer is, a lot of things. A windmill can be attached to the shaft. Wind can then rotate the coil. Water flowing downhill, steam from a boiler, or a gas engine can also be used to rotate the coil.

As a last resort, you can put a crank on the end of a generator shaft. A crank lets you turn the wire coil by hand to generate a little electricity.

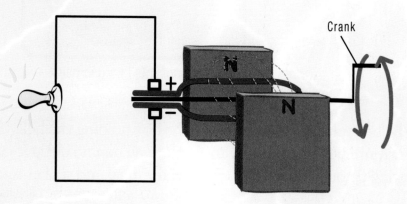

With a crank on the end of the shaft, you can generate electricity by hand.

Doorbells

When a **doorbell** button is pressed, it completes a circuit and you hear the loud "r-r-r-r-r-ing." The button is a switch. The sound comes from a bell being hit by a little hammer. It is called a **striker.** But the striker does not hit the bell just once. It hits the bell dozens of times a second. How does a doorbell work?

A doorbell has a number of components that make a circuit. It has an electricity source, a doorbell button (the switch), a box **terminal,** a striker terminal, a movable striker, an electromagnet, and a bell connected to the box. Find these parts in the drawing below.

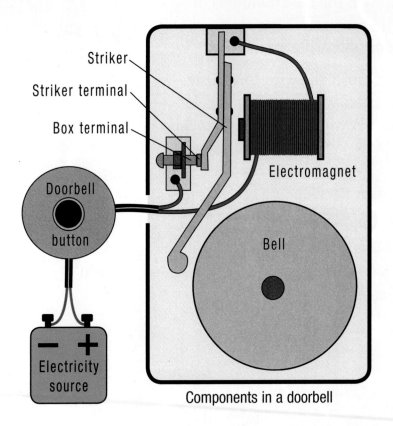

Striker

Striker terminal

Box terminal

Doorbell button

Electromagnet

Bell

Electricity source

Components in a doorbell

The box terminal is attached to the box holding the bell. The striker terminal is attached to the striker. When no electric current is flowing through the circuit, the box terminal and striker terminal touch.

When you press the doorbell button, current flows from the electricity source through the contact between the box terminal and the striker terminal. Then current flows through the striker, to the electromagnet, and back to the electricity source. The dotted lines show the path.

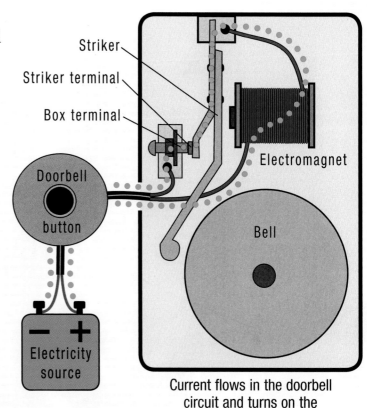

Current flows in the doorbell circuit and turns on the electromagnet.

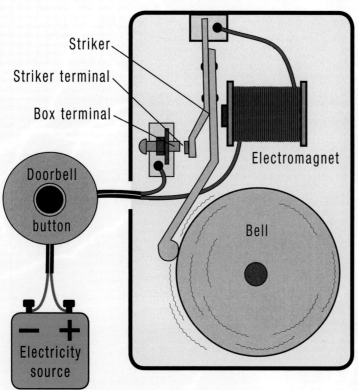

The electromagnet attracts the striker. The bell rings. The striker terminal gets pulled away from the box terminal. The circuit is broken. The magnetism goes away. The striker goes back to touch the box terminal.

When the electromagnet attracts the striker, two things happen. The striker hits the bell. And the striker terminal gets pulled away from the box terminal. This breaks the circuit. When the circuit is broken, the magnetism goes away. The striker returns to its starting position. That brings the terminals back together, so the circuit is complete. The whole process starts over. The bell rings as long as you hold the button.

Earphones

Speakers convert electric energy into motion. You may have felt the **vibrations** from speakers when music is playing. How does a speaker convert electric energy into motion?

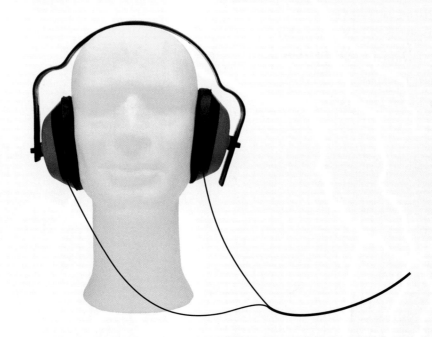

Sound from a radio starts in the form of electricity. The electric signal travels along a speaker wire to the speaker. The speaker wire is actually two wires. The sound signal travels to the speaker and back to make a complete circuit.

A speaker has two main parts. Part 1 is a coil of insulated wire glued to a paper speaker cone. Part 2 is a permanent magnet.

The permanent magnet is placed in the center of the cone.

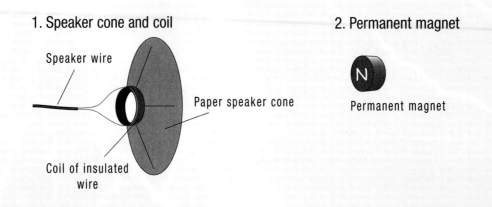

1. Speaker cone and coil

Speaker wire

Paper speaker cone

Coil of insulated wire

2. Permanent magnet

N

Permanent magnet

When a pulse of electricity flows through the coil, it creates a magnetic field. The magnetic field of the coil and the magnetic field of the permanent magnet repel. Because the coil is glued to the speaker cone, the cone moves. The movement of the cone pushes on air. This produces sound.

If you put two little speakers in the ear cups of a headset, you have a pair of **earphones.**

What if current flowing in a wire did not produce a magnetic field? How would your life be different without electromagnets?

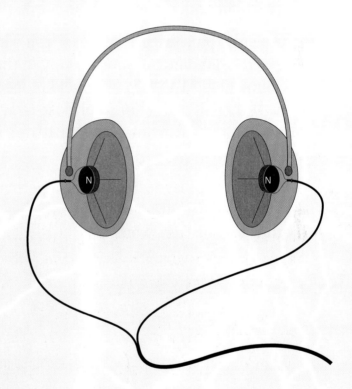

Review Questions

1. **How does a motor work?**

2. **How does a doorbell make a continuous ring?**

3. **How does a speaker work?**

4. **Give examples of devices that convert electrical energy into heat. Into light. Into sound. Into motion.**

Summary: Click It

What if current flowing in a wire did not produce a magnetic field? The modern world would be a very different place because there would be no electromagnets. Morse would not have invented his **telegraph.** Things that operate with electric **motors** would not exist. There would be no music **speakers** or **earphones.** And the junkyard crane would not be able to lift and drop discarded cars.

An electromagnet is a piece of iron with insulated wire wrapped around it. Current flowing in the wire produces a magnetic field. The magnetic field induces magnetism in the iron. If there is a piece of steel close by when the current is turned on, the electromagnet will attract it. This is how doorbells and telegraphs work.

If an electromagnet is close to a permanent magnet, the two magnets will either attract or repel each other. This is how motors and speakers work.

Electromagnets and permanent magnets can attract.

What if a wire passing through a magnetic field did not produce an electric current in the wire? For one thing, **generators** would not make electricity. There would be no place at school or home to plug in a lamp or television.

But current flowing in a wire *does* produce a magnetic field. And a wire passing through a magnetic field does produce current electricity. This makes it easy to **convert** electricity into magnetism and magnetism into electricity. And electricity, we know, can be converted into many other forms of energy: heat, sound, light, and motion.

Summary Questions

Now is a good time to review what you have recorded in your science notebook. Think about the ways you have built and used electromagnets in circuits.

1. **What causes the core of an electromagnet to become a magnet?**

2. **Discuss how an electromagnet can act as an energy converter.**

California Science Standards

PS1d. Students know the role of electromagnets in the construction of electric motors, electric generators, and simple devices, such as doorbells and earphones.

PS1g. Students know electrical energy can be converted to heat, light, and motion.

Vocabulary

telegraph

motor

speaker

earphone

generator

convert

Learning More about Magnetism and Electricity

Extensions with Magnets

Brainstorm a List

Make a list of things that might happen if you were a magnet. Think about the things a magnet might stick to that would take it on an adventure. For example, a refrigerator magnet might stick to a soup can that is being recycled. Off it goes...and the adventure continues.

Find Directions

Get a magnetic compass. Figure out how to use it for finding directions. Find out how the compass reacts when it is placed on a piece of steel. Why would it be a bad idea to place the compass on the hood of a car while attempting to determine directions?

Conduct More Force Investigations

Find out more about the strength of the force of magnetism. What will happen to the force of attraction between two magnets as more and more steel *washers* are placed between the attracting magnets? What will happen to the force of attraction between two magnets as more and more *magnets* are placed between the attracting magnets? Design an investigation. Then gather the data, prepare a chart, and report your findings.

Explore Different Magnets

Get an assortment of magnets (large, small, bar-shaped). Identify the north and south pole on each magnet. Compare the strength of the forces of attraction.

Extensions with Electric Circuits

Make a Poster

Make a poster that tells a story about electricity. Pick a theme, such as safety with electricity, where electricity comes from, or insulators and conductors.

Imagine No Electricity

Think about what daily life would be like without electricity. Find out how people who live without electricity solve problems that require a power source. Think about the advantages of not having electricity. Write a report about one or more of these ideas.

Read *Dear Mr. Henshaw*

Dear Mr. Henshaw is a book about a boy who moves to a new place and has trouble making friends. He decides to make a lunchbox alarm after the best parts of his lunch keep disappearing. Try making a lunchbox alarm for an end-of-the-module project.

Name That Insulator...Name That Conductor

This name game can be played with three or more friends. One person names an object. The next person identifies it as a conductor or an insulator. That person then names a new object. Keep the game going around the circle.

Examine the Inside of a Lightbulb

Get a bulb that has burned out. Ask an adult to put it in a bag and break the globe. Discard the glass. Look closely for the wires that connect the filament to the base and sides of the metal part of the bulb. Draw the path taken by electricity as it flows through a lightbulb.

Build a Flashlight

Get two D-cells, a lightbulb like the ones in the kit, a cardboard tube, some wire, and a roll of masking tape. Design and build a flashlight. Compare it to a real flashlight.

Find Evidence for Flow of Electricity

Set up a motor circuit. Put a black dot on one side of a flag attached to the motor shaft. Change the orientation of the D-cell and watch the flag closely. Write an explanation of your observations.

Research Inventors

Research inventors, such as Thomas Edison and Ben Franklin, who have contributed to the use of electricity in everyday life.

Make a Light Dimmer

Graphite, the black substance used as pencil lead, is a form of carbon. Graphite is a pretty good conductor, but not as good as most metals. Graphite adds resistance to the circuit. The greater the distance a current flows through graphite, the lower the current.

A bulb shines brightest when there is no resistance in the circuit with it. When resistance is added, the current goes down and the brightness of the bulb decreases.

Make a light dimmer with a no. 2 pencil by cutting the wood away on one side. Complete a circuit with different lengths of graphite in the circuit.

Safety Note: Have an adult cut the wood.

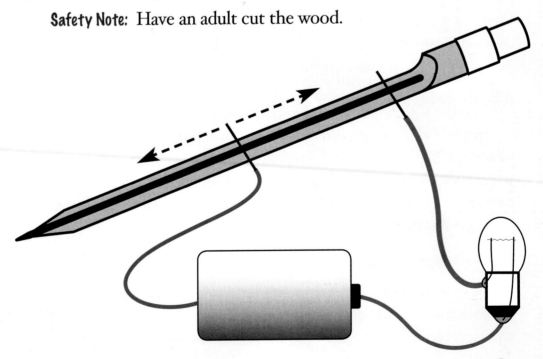

Make a Burglar Alarm

A circuit with a light can be turned into a silent burglar alarm. Cut a rectangle about 3 centimeters by 5 centimeters (1 inch by 2 inches) from an index card. Punch a hole in the rectangle and tie a piece of string to it. The string should be about 1 meter (about 3 feet) long.

Make a closed circuit that includes a lightbulb in a holder. Insert the card under the base of the bulb. This will break the circuit, and the light will go out. But if something pulls on the string, the card will slip out. This will close the circuit. The light will turn on.

Tape the free end of the string to a closed door. When the door opens, the light will go on. You have a "burglar!"

Can you use the motor to make an alarm that you can hear?

Extensions with Electromagnets

Detect Magnetism around Wires Carrying Current

Wrap the electromagnet wire around a compass that is taped to a square piece of cardboard. The cardboard should be slightly larger than the compass. Connect the wire to a complete circuit and watch the compass needle. The compass needle moves when electricity runs through the circuit. This provides evidence that wires carrying current have a magnetic field.

Compare Magnets to Electromagnets

Compare permanent magnets to electromagnets. Does the magnetism of an electromagnet work through paper or other materials like a permanent magnet does? Do two electromagnets attract and repel like permanent magnets? Does it matter which way the wire is wound on the core? Can you measure the strength of an electromagnet?

Make a Model Motor

Here is how to make a demonstration minimotor. With a bit of tinkering and some luck, the coil will spin rapidly.

1. Wrap insulated wire around a vial 20 times to make a coil. Use tape to hold it together. Bend the two ends straight out from the coil as illustrated. Remove insulation from the extended ends of the wire.

2. Bend two large paper clips as shown to make supports for the coil. Insert the paper clips into the cell holder, so that each clip contacts one end of the cell.

3. Stick a strong magnet to the cell.

4. Place the coil on the paper-clip supports and give it a little flip.

5. Fine-tuning the model motor can be tricky. Don't give up.

Build a Cardboard Telegraph

Make your own telegraph to take home. Ask your teacher for a list of materials and a set of instructions.

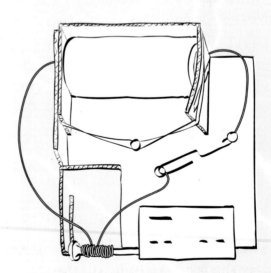

Physical Sciences Glossary

Attract   To pull toward one another.

Circuit   A pathway for the flow of electricity.

Closed circuit   A complete circuit through which electricity flows.

Code   A set of signals that represents letters or words for sending messages.

Coil   In an electromagnet, wire wound repeatedly around a central core.

Compass   An instrument that uses a free-rotating magnetic needle to show direction.

Component   One item in a circuit.

Conductor   A substance through which electricity will flow. Metals are conductors.

Contact   The place in a circuit where connections are made to allow electricity to flow.

Convert   To change.

Core   In an electromagnet, the material around which a coil of insulated wire is wound.

Current electricity   A flow of electric charge.

Doorbell   A device that uses an electromagnet to ring a bell.

Earphones   A set of two tiny speakers in a headset.

Electrically neutral   An object with equal numbers of positive and negative charges.

Electric current   A flow of electricity through a conductor.

Electric energy   A form of energy available in current electricity.

Electromagnet   A piece of iron that becomes a temporary magnet when electricity flows through an insulated wire wrapped around it.

Electron   A tiny particle with negative charge that goes around the nucleus of an atom.

Energy   Energy is the ability to do work. Energy can take a number of forms and can be converted from one form to another.

Energy conversion   Energy change from one form to another.

Filament   The material in a lightbulb (usually a thin wire) that makes light when heated by an electric current.

Force   A push or a pull.

Generator   A device that converts motion into electric energy.

Heat energy   A form of energy.

Induced magnetism   The influence of a magnetic field on a piece of iron, which makes the iron a temporary magnet.

Insulator   A material that prevents the flow of electricity. Plastic, rubber, glass, and air are insulators.

Interact   To act on and be acted upon by one or more objects.

Iron   A metal that sticks to a magnet.

Key   A switch that completes the circuit in a telegraph system.

Lightbulb   A filament held by two stiff wires and surrounded by a clear glass globe.

Light energy   A form of energy.

Lodestone   A form of the mineral magnetite that is magnetic.

Magnet   An object that sticks to iron.

Magnetic field   An invisible field around a magnet.

Magnetism   A property of certain kinds of materials that causes them to attract iron or steel.

Magnetite   An iron-rich mineral that sticks to a magnet.

Motion energy   A form of energy.

Motor   A device that converts electric energy into motion energy.

Negative charge   The charge on an electron.

North pole   The end of a magnet that orients toward Earth's magnetic north pole.

Open circuit   An incomplete circuit through which electricity will not flow.

Orient   To position an object in a certain way.

Parallel circuit   A circuit with two or more pathways for current to flow.

Permanent magnet   An object that sticks to iron.

Pole   Either of the two ends of a magnet.

Positive charge   The charge on an atom's nucleus.

Repel   To push away from one another.

Schematic diagram   A system of lines and symbols used to represent a circuit.

Series circuit   A circuit with only one pathway for current flow.

Short circuit   A circuit allowing current to flow directly from one end of a battery to the other.

South pole   The end of a magnet that orients toward Earth's magnetic south pole.

Speaker   A device that converts electric energy into motion.

Static electricity   Positive and negative electric charges that are separated from each other and are not moving.

Striker   A tiny hammer that hits the bell in a doorbell.

Telegraph   A device that uses an electromagnet to send coded messages by closing and opening an electric circuit.

Temporary magnet   A piece of iron that behaves like a magnet only when it is surrounded by a magnetic field. A temporary magnet can be a piece of iron that is touching a permanent magnet. A temporary magnet can be an electromagnet.

Terminal   An electric contact point.

Transfer   To move from one place or thing to another place or thing.

Vibration   A quick back-and-forth movement.

Life Sciences

Environments

Life Sciences
Table of Contents

Environments

Investigation 1: Terrestrial Environments

Investigation 2: Isopods and Beetles

Investigation 3: Aquatic Environments

Investigation 4: Brine Shrimp Hatching

Investigation 5: Range of Tolerance

LS3a. Students know ecosystems can be characterized by their living and nonliving components.

Setting Up a Terrarium

People like having plants around. Some people grow plants in gardens. Others have plants in pots in their homes.

And some people grow plants in **terrariums.** A terrarium is a container with plants growing inside. It's a little space closed off from the rest of the world.

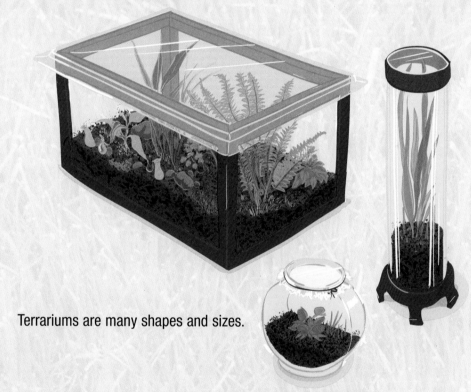

Terrariums are many shapes and sizes.

Terrariums can be any size and shape. Any clear container can be made into a terrarium. It should have a deep layer of soil and a lid to keep moisture inside. And it needs to be large enough to hold the plants you want to grow inside. A well-planned terrarium provides a good **environment** for the plants.

So what makes a good environment for a plant? It depends on the plant. All **organisms** have needs. Plants need air, water, light, and space. But not every kind of plant needs the same amount of water, light, and space. Some plants need a lot of water. Others require only a small amount. Some plants need bright light, while others grow better in the shade. Some plants grow best in cool temperatures, and others **thrive** in the heat.

An organism's environment is *everything* that surrounds and affects it. Each part or **component** of an organism's environment is an **environmental factor.** An environmental factor can be **nonliving,** such as water, light, and air temperature. Environmental factors also can be **living,** like all the plants and animals surrounding an organism.

So, when making a terrarium, you need to think about the environmental factors for the plants that will grow in it. What kind of soil will you use? Will you have one kind of plant or several kinds? How much water will you give the plants and how often? Will the lid stay on the container or come off? Where should the terrarium be placed in the room for light and temperature?

Review Questions

1. **What is an environmental factor? Give some examples.**

2. **The word *terra* means earth or land. The suffix *-arium* means a place. Write a definition for the word *terrarium*.**

3. **What do you think these words mean? Aquarium? Vivarium?**

HOMEMADE TERRARIUM

In class, you made a terrarium in a clear plastic container. You can make your own terrarium at home out of a recycled 2-liter clear plastic soda bottle. Here's how.

What You Need

1 2-liter plastic bottle

- Soil

- Gravel or pebbles

- Seeds or small plants

- Scissors

- Water

What You Do

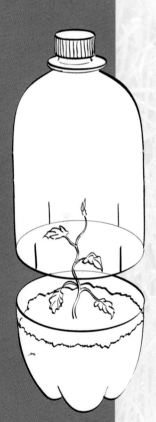

1. Remove the label from the soda bottle. With help from an adult, cut the bottle about 10 centimeters (4 inches) from the bottom. Leave the cap on the bottle.

2. Cut four 2-centimeter (1-inch) slits along the bottom edge of the top part of the bottle.

3. Put a layer of gravel or small pebbles in the base. Add a layer of soil. If you are planting seeds in the terrarium, fill the base with soil almost to the top. Then plant your seeds.

   If you are planting a small rooted plant, dig a hole in the soil. Place the roots of the plant in the hole. Fill soil in around the roots.

4. Water the soil.

5. Place the top section of your bottle on the base, fitting the slits over the base. Place the terrarium in a well-lit area. See how your plants grow in their environment.

INVESTIGATION 1

LS3a. Students know ecosystems can be characterized by their living and nonliving components.

Two Terrestrial Environments

Environmental scientists know a lot about Earth's environments. They have named six different major **terrestrial** environments. Terrestrial refers to Earth's land. (The other environments on Earth are water environments.) The six terrestrial environments are **tropical rain forest, desert, temperate deciduous forest, grassland, taiga,** and **tundra.**

The main nonliving components that define the six environments are temperature, rainfall, and soil type. For example, deserts are dry and sandy. Any area on Earth that is dry and sandy is a desert environment. Most deserts are hot, but some are cold. There are deserts on five continents. Deserts in Africa are different from deserts in southern California. But both environments are deserts because they are dry and sandy.

The tropical rain forest environment is different from the desert environment. The tropical rain forest is hot and wet, and the soil is poor. Let's take a closer look at these two terrestrial environments and compare the nonliving and living components.

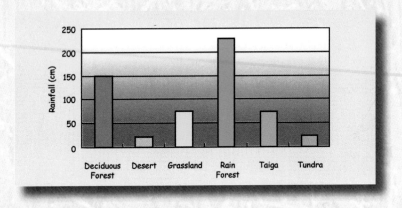

Average rainfall in six terrestrial environments

Deserts

Some people think of deserts as hot, dry wastelands. Sometimes this is true. Huge areas of shifting sand, such as the Sahara of Africa, don't support much life. Other deserts are full of life. The Mojave Desert of southern California is rich with plants and animals. What's the difference? Why does life struggle to survive in some deserts and thrive in others?

Sand dune in the Sahara (right)

Mojave Desert in California (bottom)

Scientists define desert as any place on Earth that receives less than 25 centimeters (10 inches) of rain per year. Soils are rocky or sandy in deserts. Water runs off the land quickly or sinks into the sand. Water **evaporates** or dries up quickly in the desert. Much of the small amount of water that does fall on the desert is lost before plants and animals can get to it. Look at the map to see where deserts are on Earth.

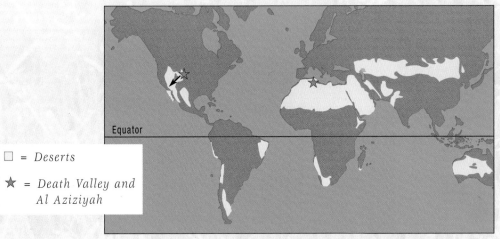

☐ = Deserts

★ = Death Valley and Al Aziziyah

Equator

Deserts are found north and south of the equator.

Deserts are the hottest places on Earth. The highest temperature ever recorded was 58°C (136°F) in Al Aziziyah, in the North African country of Libya. The second highest temperature, 57°C (135°F), was recorded in Death Valley, California. During the winter, the temperatures can drop below freezing. Snow is seen regularly in parts of the deserts in southern California, China, and South America.

In California deserts, the average summer temperature is 35°C (95°F). The average winter temperature is 13°C (55°F). The overall average temperature is 24°C (75°F).

About 20 percent of Earth's land surface is desert. The small amount of rain, high temperatures, and large temperature changes from season to season make life challenging in the desert.

Snow on Joshua trees in the Mojave Desert

Fewer kinds of plants and animals live in deserts than in wetter environments. Desert plants and animals have **structures** and **behaviors** that help them to survive in this environment.

In deserts, some plants grow far apart. Their root systems spread over a large area. This lets them get water and nutrients without **competition** from other plants. Some desert plants, such as the mesquite tree, send their roots deep into the desert soil. Mesquite roots may go down 81 meters (267 feet) to reach water.

Widely spaced desert plants

Barrel cactus

Cacti store water in their broad, fleshy blades or columns, which are actually stems. They use the stored water during long dry periods. The seeds of some desert plants can lie in the soil for years until it rains enough for them to **sprout.**

Animals survive well in the southern California deserts. Insects, spiders, reptiles, birds, and mammals live in deserts. Many desert animals are **nocturnal.** Nocturnal animals stay out of the midday heat by coming out only at night. During the day, they remain in the shade or in **burrows** dug into the desert soil. Many desert animals, such as the kangaroo rat, have bodies that conserve water. They do not sweat, and their urine isn't liquid, it's solid. Other animals, such as the desert bighorn sheep, get most of their water from the food they eat.

Desert tortoises are completely at home in the desert. They dig deep burrows. When it is too hot or too cold, they have a safe place to stay. Tortoises eat many kinds of plants, especially their flowers and fruits. Sometimes they will even eat the moist pads of cactus plants. Tortoises drink a lot of water when they can and store it in their bladders.

Spadefoot toads are **amphibians.** That means they have to **reproduce** in water. Is the desert a good place for them to live?

A desert tortoise

Desert bighorn sheep

A spadefoot toad

Yes. When the weather is hot and dry, the toads burrow about a meter (3 feet) underground. They can stay there for up to 9 months. They become inactive and live on the fat stored in their bodies. When it rains, spadefoot toads leave their burrows and find mates. The females lay eggs in rain puddles. The eggs soon hatch into tadpoles. The tadpoles grow into young toads. The young toads have to become adults before the puddles dry up or they will die. In a couple of months, the survivors burrow down into the ground and wait for next year's rain.

Every desert animal and plant has structures and behaviors that allow it to survive and even thrive in the hot, dry desert.

Tropical Rain Forests

Tropical rain forests are home to more kinds of life than any other terrestrial environment. At least half of all the different kinds of plants and animals in the world live in tropical rain forests. Tropical rain forests are also the winter homes for many birds that live in other places the rest of the year.

Look at the map. It is green where tropical rain forests are. Can you find the ones in Australia? In Asia? In Africa? In Central America? In South America? Where else are there tropical forests? Find the line that shows the equator.

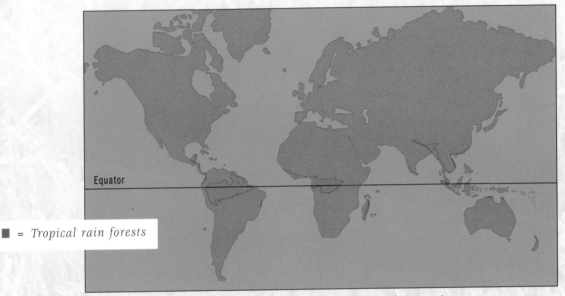

Equator

■ = *Tropical rain forests*

Tropical rain forests are found near the equator.

Tropical rain forests are wet all year. The rainfall in rain forests is about 200 to 450 centimeters (80 to 180 inches) per year. How does that compare to where you live? Here are average rainfalls for four California cities.

San Diego = 33 cm (13 inches)

Los Angeles = 28 cm (11 inches)

Sacramento = 45 cm (18 inches)

San Francisco = 45 cm (18 inches)

Tropical rain forests are hot all year. In the coolest months, the average temperature is about 25°C (77°F). In the warmest months, the average temperature is about 35°C (95°F). What is the difference in temperature between the cool and hot months?

Living Components

Life in the rain forest can be divided into layers. Each layer has different plants and animals. Most of the tropical rain forest plants are trees. They grow to heights of 20 to 30 meters (66 to 99 feet). Because the trees grow very close to one another, their tops grow together. This forms a broad **canopy,** or roof, above the forest.

The highest layer in the rain forest is the forest canopy. There is a lot of sunlight in the canopy layer. This is where most of the rain forest animals live. Monkeys, sloths, and bats spend most of their time here. Tree frogs and snakes live here along with toucans, hummingbirds, ants, and beetles. These are just a few of the millions of different kinds of animals that live in the canopy. Orchids, ferns, and other "air plants" grow on the branches of the canopy trees. Air plants use the tree for support and get water from the falling rain.

The layer below the canopy is the **understory.** Little sunlight makes it through the canopy to the understory. It is a dark place full of tree trunks, young thin trees, and broad-leafed plants that can live in shady conditions. A number of these plants are popular house plants in California. The animals living in this layer include jaguars, leopards, frogs, snakes, parakeets, and many kinds of insects.

The bottom layer is the **forest floor.** The forest floor is often covered with moss and wet leaves. Very little light makes it to the floor. This is where centipedes and scorpions live. Many insects, such as termites, ants, cockroaches, and beetles, also live here. Earthworms and fungi use the dead leaves as food. Larger animals, such as tapirs, dig up roots in the forest floor.

Can you identify the frog, tapir, toucan, and monkey?

The rain forest soil is shallow and not very **fertile.** Most of the **nutrients** (raw materials) that plants need to survive are in the trees. If the trees are cut down and taken away, the nutrients are lost to the rain forest environment. This is why it takes a long time for tropical rain forests to grow back once they are destroyed. But if the tree dies in the forest, the nutrients can be broken down and **recycled** into the soil.

One hundred years ago, rain forests covered a much larger area than they do now. Today trees are cut down and burned to make new farmland. Trees are also cut for lumber and to clear land for mining.

Rain forest cleared for farming

The loss of rain forest is a concern to everyone in the world. Eighty percent of the organisms in tropical rain forests have not been named. Some live in very small areas that are hard to get to. Scientists worry that these organisms may die out because the environment has been changed. The rain forests may have plants that could provide humans with sources of medicine. These plants could be lost if the rain forests are destroyed.

Review Questions

1. What are the environmental factors that define a desert environment?

2. What are the environmental factors that define a tropical rain forest environment?

3. Compare the environmental factor of water in deserts and rain forests.

4. Make a bar graph to compare the environmental factor of temperature in deserts and rain forests.

Summary: Terrestrial Environments

Baby's tears is the name of a low-growing plant with tiny leaves. It thrives in warm, shady, moist places. It can live nicely in a **terrarium.** To set up the terrarium for baby's tears, you might put soil, rocks, and water in a clear container. When you are done, you have an **environment** for this plant.

The baby's tears plant depends on its environment for survival. The terrarium is a small **terrestrial** environment. The soil, water, air temperature, and light in the terrarium are **environmental factors** that affect the plant. If the factors are right, over time you will see the plant grow and thrive.

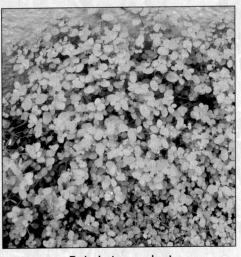

Baby's tears plant

A terrarium for plants

Most plants don't live in terrariums. They live in natural environments. Tropical rain forests are one natural environment. Rain forests are wet and hot all year. **Organisms** that can live in hot, wet environments live in rain forests. Rain forests are defined by their **living** and **nonliving components.**

Deserts are another kind of natural environment. The desert environments are dry. During the summer, deserts are hot. During the winter, they are cool. Plants and animals that can live in hot and cold, dry environments live in deserts. Deserts are also defined by their living and nonliving components.

You can buy baby's tears at a nursery. But the nursery is not the natural environment for baby's tears. Somewhere baby's tears is growing in its natural environment. If you know the environment in which baby's tears thrives, you will know how to set up the nonliving components in the terrarium.

Summary Questions

Now is a good time to review what you have recorded in your science notebook. Think about the investigations you have conducted with terrariums.

1. Do you think baby's tears can live in a rain forest or a desert? Explain why you think so.

2. Describe the living and nonliving components of the environment in the terrarium you made in class.

3. Do you think baby's tears could live in your classroom terrarium? Explain why or why not.

California Science Standard

LS3a. Students know ecosystems can be characterized by their living and nonliving components.

Vocabulary

terrarium
environment
terrestrial
environmental factor
organism
living
nonliving
component

Extensions

Math Problem of the Week

Eric, José, Shannon, and Jackie want to plant a garden. Jackie's dad said they could use an area in their backyard that was an 8 meters by 4 meters rectangle.

• Fair Plots: The friends want to divide the area into four equal parts. Each friend has a different way to divide the garden plot fairly. Show at least four different ways the garden could be divided. Which one would you pick for the garden? Why?

• How Much Area to Plant? The friends voted and have a garden plan. Eric wants to know how much area each person has to plant. Jackie calculated and said that each would get 12 square meters to plant. José said they would each get 8 square meters. Shannon said they would get 8 meters each. Jackie's dad said only one of the friends had the correct answer.

What is the area of each person's piece of the garden? Show how you determined your answer.

• A Row of Marigolds: The friends decided to plant a single row of marigolds along one of the 8 meter sides. They will start the row at one corner of the garden plot and plant to the opposite corner. Marigolds need to be planted 10 centimeters apart. How many marigolds will they need for the row?

• A Border for the Garden: The friends really like the row of marigolds along one side of the garden. They want to plant marigolds around the whole garden. The border of marigolds will be planted along the outer edges or the perimeter of the garden. How many marigolds will they need in all to make a border for the garden? Show all your work.

Home/School Connection

Make a list of living and nonliving environmental factors found in and around your home. Discuss the list with a family member. Does he or she agree? Select one item you disagree on. Write a brief explanation telling why you think the environmental factor is living or nonliving.

LS3b. Students know that in any particular environment, some kinds of plants and animals survive well, some survive less well, and some cannot survive at all.

Isopods and Beetles

Isopods

R oly-poly bugs! Sow bugs! These are two common names people give to **isopods.** But isopods aren't bugs at all. *Iso* means "similar" or "equal," and *pod* means "foot." So the scientific name tells us that the isopod's seven pairs of legs are all the same.

The reason isopods are not bugs is that they have seven pairs of legs. True bugs are **insects,** and all insects have *three* pairs of legs.

All seven pairs of isopod legs have the same **function.** Isopods use all seven pairs of legs for walking, and nothing else. Insect legs are used for many functions. These include feeding, grasping, jumping, swimming, and carrying. This is another way isopods are different from insects.

Isopods

There are many kinds of isopods, but all are **crustaceans.** Crustaceans are animals with shells, jaws, and two pairs of **antennae.** Crustaceans include crabs, shrimps, and lobsters. Most crustaceans live in water and breathe with **gills.** Isopods are a little different. They can live on land. But they have to be in a moist environment most of the time. As long as they keep their gill-like breathing structures wet, they can breathe. If these structures become dry, the isopod cannot survive.

Did you observe two different kinds of isopods in class? One kind is dome-shaped and has short antennae. When this isopod is in danger, it can roll up into a ball. That's why it is called a **pill bug.**

Pill bugs

The other isopod is flatter and has longer antennae. It is called a **sow bug.** A sow bug cannot roll up to protect itself from a hungry spider or insect. But it can run faster than a pill bug.

A sow bug

Sow bugs and pill bugs feed on dead leaves. They play an important role in recycling dead plant material.

Darkling Beetles

Darkling beetles are insects. They live in almost every part of the world, from the desert to the rain forest. There are many different kinds. In North America alone, there are 1,400 kinds of darkling beetles! One kind of darkling beetle is the *Tenebrio.*

The adult *Tenebrio* beetle is about 1.9 centimeters (0.7 inches) long. It is dark brown to black and usually lives in dark, dry places. Like other insects, the *Tenebrio* darkling beetle has six legs and three body parts. These parts are the head, thorax, and abdomen. Like other beetles, it has two pairs of wings. The front wings cover and protect the back wings and abdomen. But darkling beetles cannot fly.

The darkling beetle goes through four stages in its life cycle. The stages are **egg, larva, pupa,** and **adult** beetle. Female beetles lay 500 to 1,000 eggs at a time. The eggs hatch in about a week. For about a week after hatching, the larvae are too small to be seen.

The larvae of *Tenebrio* beetles are yellow-gold in color. They are called **mealworms,** but they are not worms at all. The larvae eat cereals and grains. They grow to a length of 3 centimeters (1.25 inches).

A *Tenebrio* beetle

The larvae molt (shed their tough outer skin) several times in order to grow. After about 3 months, the larvae change into pupae.

The pupa is a resting stage. The insect's body begins to change into an adult beetle. The pupa stage lasts about 2 weeks. Then the beetle comes out as an adult. This cycle of changes is called **complete metamorphosis.**

In the natural environment, *Tenebrio* beetles live in grasslands where there are plenty of seeds. They also make their homes near humans. They get into cupboards, pantries, and chicken farms. For this reason, darkling beetles might be thought of as pests. But they are harmless.

Larvae (mealworms)

A pupa

Other Beetles

What makes a beetle a beetle? The most important characteristic that all beetles share is their short, hard front wings called elytra. When a beetle folds its wings, the elytra cover its entire abdomen. This shell gives a beetle its "armored" appearance. When a beetle flies, it lifts its elytra so that its back wings can beat.

All beetles go through the same four stages of growth as the darkling beetle. Females lay eggs that hatch into wormlike larvae. The larvae eat, grow, and pupate. Finally, the pupae change into adults. At least 250,000 kinds of beetles have been described by scientists. Beetles can be less than a centimeter (0.5 inch) to more than 15 centimeters (6 inches) long.

Another kind of darkling beetle

Beetles live in just about every environment on Earth. They live in rain forests, deserts, mountain lakes, rivers, and northern forests. They can live in people's homes and gardens. They can even live in sewers. The only environment they don't live in is the ocean.

Beetles eat almost everything. Some eat leaves, fruit, bark, seeds, and grains. Others are **parasites** and live on or in living animals. Some beetles are **scavengers,** living on dead animals or dung. Beetles can be helpful to humans. For example, beetles called ladybugs are **predators.** They eat small insects that destroy garden and farm plants.

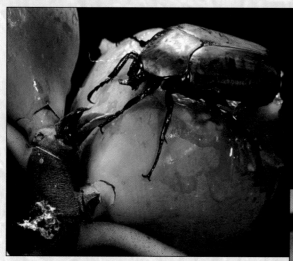

A metallic green fig beetle

A ten lined June beetle

What group of insects do you think is the most successful on Earth? Flies? Mosquitoes? Ants? It's the beetles. There are more kinds of beetles than all the other kinds of insects added together.

1 million

And how many different kinds of insects are there? About 1 million of the 1.5 million kinds of organisms that have been described by scientists are insects. The list of insects is growing at the rate of about 7,000 to 10,000 new kinds every year! Based on work done in rain forests, some scientists think there may be 10 to 30 million more kinds of insects to discover. The estimated 260,000 kinds of plants, 20,000 fish, 8,600 birds, 7,500 reptiles, and 4,000 mammals seem quite small compared to the millions of insects.

Review Questions

1. **What kind of environment do isopods need to survive well? Why?**

2. **How can you tell if a small animal is a beetle?**

3. **What does this bar graph tell you about the estimated numbers of different kinds of organisms on Earth?**

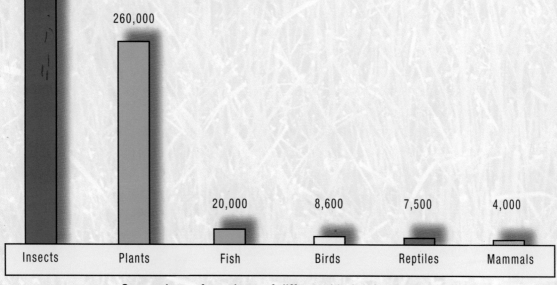

260,000

20,000   8,600   7,500   4,000

| Insects | Plants | Fish | Birds | Reptiles | Mammals |

Comparison of numbers of different kinds of organisms

INVESTIGATION 2

LS3a. Students know ecosystems can be characterized by their living and nonliving components.

Amazon Rain Forest Journal

My name is Lee. My mother is an **entomologist.** That's a biologist who studies insects. She has traveled to the Amazon River in Brazil many times. Her stories about the rain forest always sounded so exciting. I begged Mom for a long time to take me on one of her trips to the rain forest. Finally, she surprised me with a special birthday trip. I wrote a journal about my trip to share my experiences with everyone at school.

Monday, July 21

It's early morning, and I am sitting in the Manaus Airport in Brazil. I can't believe that I'm so far from Los Angeles, 10,880 kilometers (almost 6,800 miles)!

We are waiting for a small plane to take us down the Amazon River to the city of Santarém. That's where the ecology research station is. Mom is one of more than 100 scientists who work there.

It's early afternoon now. The flight was great. The forest below looked like a green carpet as far as I could see. Mom's friend Kopenawa met us at the airport. She has known Kopenawa for a long time. He has guided her safely through the forest many times. He was ready to take us for a short hike in the rain forest. Mom says he knows more about the rain forest environment than almost anyone else.

We're going down the biggest river in the world. Once the boat moved away from the city, I knew I was in a new environment. The air was really hot and humid. I could feel sweat soaking my clothes. Everything I saw was huge! The trees are the tallest I've ever seen, and there are interesting plants with gigantic leaves everywhere I look.

After traveling a short distance, Kopenawa guided the boat over to the riverbank. We're going into the forest!

We are back in Kopenawa's boat after a short hike in the rain forest. From the riverbank, the forest looked really dense. I didn't think we would be able to walk through it. But it was much easier to walk when we got away from the river and into the trees. Mom said this is because the tops of the trees form a canopy, or cover. Only a little light can make it through the canopy, so fewer plants actually grow on the forest floor.

I saw my first rain forest animal. It was a big lizard like this one. I nearly stepped on it because it blended in so well with the plants. Kopenawa said the lizard's camouflage makes it very hard for predators to see. It was hard for me to see, too.

Tuesday, July 22

After our short walk in the rain forest yesterday, Kopenawa took us on to the research station. We have a little room in a cabin with just screens on the windows. The sounds of the forest birds and monkeys woke me up early. I ate breakfast in a room full of long tables. Scientists were talking about rainfall, soil, temperature, seed sprouting, parrots, beetles, and a lot more. I was ready to find out more for myself.

A short distance from the cabin I saw a line of thousands of very large ants. They were marching through the rain forest on a trail they made. When I got closer, I could see that many of the ants held pieces of green leaves over their heads. They looked like they were carrying tiny umbrellas. They really looked funny. I asked Kopenawa if they were protecting themselves from the rain. He laughed and told me that they were leaf-cutter ants. They cut circles out of leaves and carry them back to their underground nests. Their nests are made of hundreds of small rooms, called chambers, under the earth.

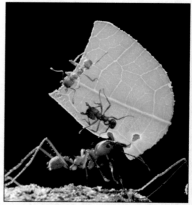
Leaf-cutter ant

The leaf-cutter ants don't eat the leaves. In fact, some of the leaves are poisonous. The ants use the leaves to grow a type of fungus. They chew the leaves. This makes a bed of leaf pulp where the fungus grows. The fungus is what the ants eat.

I asked Kopenawa if the ants ever get lost in the forest. The ground is covered with roots, rocks, and plants. I thought they must have trouble finding their way home. Kopenawa explained that the ants put down drops of a chemical, called a pheromone. The pheromones mark the trail for other ants to follow.

Leaf-cutter ants

Ants reproduce with complete metamorphosis, like beetles. The queen ant lays eggs that hatch into larvae. The adult ants feed fungus to the larvae until the larvae pupate. Soon after, the adults come out. The new ants are called workers. They get right to work cutting leaves and growing fungus.

We kept walking. In half an hour, Kopenawa stopped and pointed to a spot near the trail. More ants! But this time, a battle was going on. A group of red army ants was attacking a group of wasps. Army ants do not eat leaves or fungus. They eat other insects such as wasps, moths, and hoppers. Wasps and ants are called social insects because they live together in groups. We watched the ants swarm over the wasps' nest. There were so many army ants that the wasps could not defend themselves. The wasps could only fly away and leave their larvae and eggs behind. The ants carried the wasp eggs and larvae back to their own nest. The eggs and larvae would be food for the rest of the ants.

A short distance away, we saw a ball of army ants the size of a basketball. Kopenawa said the ants were making a temporary nest. This is the only kind of nest they ever make. The ants hook themselves together in chains. The chains form chambers for the queen and growing larvae. It was like something out of a science fiction movie, a living fort.

Mom told me that the army ants have to keep moving. They eat all the insects and other small animals in their path. They need to keep finding new places to get food.

Wednesday, July 23

Today we got up very early and went for a hike right after breakfast. Suddenly Kopenawa put out his hand and stopped me in my tracks. A coral snake was slithering through the leaves on the ground. The snake had bright bands of yellow, red, and black. Some rain forest animals are brightly colored. Often the red or yellow animals are poisonous. The color warns predators to stay away. I kept my distance. I took this photograph of the coral snake. Then the snake disappeared into the forest.

A coral snake

Thursday, July 24

Today I went with my mom to her study area. She studies plants and the insects that eat them. I was surprised to hear that most of the trees we were walking under were poisonous. Mom said that's how trees defend themselves against the millions of hungry insects in the forest. If the plants didn't have defensive chemicals, all their leaves would be eaten and they would die.

What interests Mom is why some insects are not affected by the poison leaves. Every kind of tree seems to be eaten by one or two kinds of insects. What makes it possible for those insects to eat leaves that are poison to every other kind of insect? That's what Mom tries to figure out.

Mom pointed out a small tree and warned me not to touch it. I thought it might be poisonous, but my mom said no, it was the ants that lived on it. Because this small tree grows in the forest understory, it doesn't get much light. It needs every leaf to survive. The ants attack any leaf-eating animals that come close to the tree. The ants make it possible for the tree to survive.

The small tree has hollow leaves that provide shelter for the ants. The tree also supports a number of sap-sucking insects called aphids. The aphid herds produce a sweet substance called honeydew. The ants live on the honeydew. The tree makes it possible for the ants to survive.

Seeing the ant tree reminded my mom of a tree called the swollen thorn acacia. She observed it on a study trip to the rain forest in Costa Rica in Central America. The leaves of this acacia tree are not poisonous, but the tree is not eaten by insects. It has another way to survive.

The acacia produces sugar syrup and little fruitlike bulbs. The bulbs are rich in vitamins and proteins. But, only one kind of insect, an ant, eats the abundant food. Why?

Again, the ants protect the tree! When a hungry insect lands on the acacia tree, the ants attack it. If a vine touches the tree, the ants chew through the vine and cut it from the tree. As the acacia tree grows, the ants cut away the ends of the branches on the neighboring trees.

Ants live inside these large thorns.

The large, swollen acacia thorns are hollow. The ants live safely inside the thorns.

It's amazing. The acacia tree provides food and protection for the ants, and the ants protect the tree. The tree and the ants depend on each other for survival.

Ants sipping sugar syrup

Friday, July 25

This was the best day of all. I had been looking forward to it all week. I actually went into the top of the forest today, up into the canopy. The research station has a set of walkways in the canopy. The trip to the canopy started with an elevator ride. Mom called it a "lift." The lift carried us up 30 meters (100 feet). When the lift stopped, we stepped onto a maze of walkways that stretched through the treetops. Each tree trunk had a strong wooden platform around it. The platforms were big enough for a few people to stand on them. As I looked around, I felt like I was on top of the world. We were in the rain forest canopy.

It would be hard to describe all of the animals I saw. I mostly noticed there were many kinds of birds. I saw colorful macaws and toucans. Many of the trees were covered with small berries. The branches were full of howler monkeys, dwarf squirrels, and tree frogs. I was amazed that the top of the forest was so full of life. It was very different from the forest floor.

Saturday, July 26

This was my last day in the rain forest. I spent so much time hiking around that I am too tired to write very much. Even though the weather was hot and humid and it rained every day of the trip, I didn't mind. There were so many new things to see and hear!

A toucan

A howler monkey

A scarlet macaw

A red-eyed tree frog

I'll miss Kopenawa. It was hard to say good-bye to him today. And I'll never forget all the animals, the toucans, howler monkeys, snakes, and the rest. It was amazing to see so many different kinds of plants and animals living together. Everything seems to fit together and work together. It's like fitting all the pieces of a puzzle together to make a beautiful picture. I'll keep this picture in my mind all the way back to Los Angeles.

The canopy walkway

A view from the canopy walkway

Studying the Rain Forest

Lee's mother is a type of biologist called an entomologist. She studies insects in the rain forest, particularly ants. These organisms, like many plants, animals, and fungi, can survive only in the rain forest. The cutting of trees is causing the destruction of the rain forest and the extinction of many plants and animals. Little is known about many of the organisms in the rain forest. Studying them is important because of the potential benefits this knowledge may bring to our world.

Review Questions

1. What did Lee learn about ants on his rain forest adventure?

2. How do plants and animals help each other in the rain forest?

3. In what ways do animals depend on plants in the rain forest environment? How do the plants depend on the animals in the rain forest environment?

4. What environmental factor changes as you go from the rain forest canopy to the forest floor?

LS3c. Students know many plants depend on animals for pollination and seed dispersal, and animals depend on plants for food and shelter.

How Organisms Depend on One Another

Animals depend on plants for survival. Trees provide **shelter** for birds to build nests. High in the branches, eggs and baby birds are safe from snakes, skunks, and coyotes. The little owl in the picture below is protected from weather and predators by a tall cactus. Beetles and isopods live under bark. Walkingsticks hide in twigs to protect themselves from predators. And animals depend on plants for food. Animals eat leaves, flowers, fruits, seeds, bark, stems, sap, and roots of plants. It's easy to find lots of examples of ways animals depend on plants for survival.

An elf owl nesting in a saguaro cactus

A walkingstick among twigs

Plants depend on animals for survival. You know about the swollen thorn acacia tree. The ants help the tree **survive.** If an insect lands on the tree, the ants will attack it. If another plant touches the tree, the ants cut it away. The acacia tree depends on the ants for protection. And the ants depend on the tree for shelter and food.

Pollination

What other ways do plants depend on animals? Think about honeybees visiting flowers. Bees get nectar and pollen from flowers. This is food for the bees. The bees depend on plants for food.

A bee collects pollen and nectar for food.

The plants also depend on the bees. Pollen must get from one flower to another for plants to make seeds. This is called **pollination.** Plants can't move, so the pollen must be carried from one flower to another. Bees carry pollen as they fly from flower to flower. (Can you see the yellow dust on this bee's body? That's the pollen.) Bees make it possible for plants to produce seeds. The seeds grow to become adult plants, which make flowers with nectar and pollen. Then the cycle starts over again.

Other insects, such as butterflies and moths, also visit flowers for food. Plants depend on insects to bring pollen, and insects depend on plants for food. Without bees, and other insects that visit flowers, plants cannot survive. Without flowers on plants, bees and butterflies cannot survive.

Seed Dispersal

When seeds are ripe, they are ready to grow. Seeds have a better chance of survival if they sprout away from the parent plant. The new plant will be able to get more light, water, and nutrients. **Seed dispersal** is the term used to describe ways that seeds move away from the parent plant.

Sometimes wind disperses or scatters seeds. Wind is dispersing the small seeds of this dandelion.

Dandelion seeds blowing in the wind

Animals can also disperse seeds. Squirrels, chipmunks, and birds often take seeds and fruits (acorns, sunflower seeds, berries, and cherries) for food. They may drop the seeds or bury them and forget where they put them. Seeds with hooks can also stick to animals to be carried away from the parent plant.

Animals depend on plants for survival. Plants give animals food and shelter. Plants also depend on animals for survival. Animals help pollinate plants and disperse seeds.

Sometimes birds drop the seeds they are carrying.

A chipmunk with acorns in its cheeks

Review Questions

1. **Describe three examples of how animals depend on plants for survival.**

2. **Describe three examples of how plants depend on animals for survival.**

3. **Do you think animals pollinate flowers and disperse seeds on purpose or by accident? Explain why you think so.**

Summary: Isopods and Beetles

Many of the thousands of **insects** living in the rain forest depend on plants for food and **shelter.** The question is, how do plants **survive?** With all those hungry insects around, why don't they eat up every plant in sight?

This is a question Lee's mother is trying to answer with her research in the rain forest. When she observed a tamtam tree, she saw only one kind of yellow larva eating the leaves. When she looked further, she observed that every tamtam tree had the same yellow larvae eating the leaves. Why?

Lee's mom made more observations. In her laboratory, she found that the tamtam leaves had a large amount of a poisonous chemical. She also observed that the larvae had the same poison in their bodies. Lee's mom interpreted these observations to come up with this explanation.

Over a long time, the tamtam tree developed the ability to make the poison. The poison helps the tree survive. It keeps most insects from eating it. Over time one kind of insect developed the ability to eat the leaves without harm. This ability helps the insect survive. It can eat food no other insect can eat. The poison in its body protects it from **predators.** This is one example of how a plant and an animal depend on each other for survival.

Lee's mom figured out this relationship by making observations and interpreting her observations. Most new scientific knowledge is a result of both observation and interpretation.

Scientists also use observation and interpretation to learn other ways animals help plants survive. Plants can't produce seeds unless pollen gets from one flower to another. Bees and other insects pollinate flowers as they feed on nectar. Plants depend on animals for **pollination.** After seeds develop, animals carry them away as food or on their fur or feathers. **Seed dispersal** helps plants move to new places.

You did an experiment with isopods and darkling beetles. You observed their movements to learn what kind of environment they prefer. Just like any other scientist, you made observations and interpreted them. You now have a better idea of the nonliving factors that affect isopod and darkling beetle behavior and survival.

Summary Questions

Now is a good time to review what you have recorded in your science notebook. Think about the investigations you have conducted with isopods and beetles.

1. **Why do you think Lee did not see any barrel cacti or desert bighorn sheep in the rain forest environment?**

2. **What do you think would happen if bees and butterflies disappeared from every environment?**

3. **What is seed dispersal? Why is it important?**

California Science Standards

LS3a. Students know ecosystems can be characterized by their living and nonliving components.

LS3b. Students know that in any particular environment, some kinds of plants and animals survive well, some survive less well, and some cannot survive at all.

LS3c. Students know many plants depend on animals for pollination and seed dispersal, and animals depend on plants for food and shelter.

Vocabulary

insect

shelter

survive

predator

pollination

seed dispersal

Extensions

Math Problem of the Week

Allison's Ladybug Cage

Allison made a ladybug cage. Her cage has five sides. Each side has a length of 28 centimeters. The cage is 20 centimeters high. What is the shape of her cage's base called? What is the perimeter of the base?

Josh's Beetle Cages

Josh wants to build rectangular beetle cages to study beetle behavior. He wants all the sides on the base of his cages to be at least 10 centimeters long. Josh also wants the base area to equal 576 centimeters^2.

Josh needs help to find all the possible lengths and widths for the base of the cages. Josh only used whole centimeters to measure with no fractional parts.

What are all the possible dimensions for the rectangular base?

Josh has decided to make the height of each cage 10 cm. If he fills the container to capacity, how much soil will he need for each cage?

Home/School Connection

Go on an insect safari around your home. Look for insects, like butterflies, bees, moths, grasshoppers, ladybugs, ants, flies, mosquitoes, and roaches. You might find small animals that are not insects, but live in the same environments, such as millipedes, isopods, and spiders.

Safety Note: While most insects, spiders, and other small animals are harmless, some can sting (ants, wasps, bees), and some can bite (spiders, centipedes). Observe without touching, for your safety and the well-being of the animals.

Organize the results of your safari. Identify the insects and describe their environments. Try to identify both living and nonliving factors in the organisms' environments.

LS3a. Students know ecosystems can be characterized by their living and nonliving components.

LS3b. Students know that in any particular environment, some kinds of plants and animals survive well, some survive less well, and some cannot survive at all.

FRESHWATER ENVIRONMENTS

There are two kinds of freshwater environments, standing-water environments and flowing-water environments. Lakes are the most common standing-water environments. Other standing-water environments are ponds and **vernal pools.** Rivers, streams, and creeks are flowing-water environments.

Lakes

Lakes are bodies of water surrounded by land. They are all over the world. Some lakes are low in valleys, like Lake Shasta in northern California. Others are high in mountains like Lake 12,460 shown below. It's high in the Sierra Nevada range in California.

Lake 12,460 in Sequoia National Park, California

Less than 1 percent of Earth's water is in freshwater lakes. Although lakes are called standing-water environments, the water in lakes is always moving. Water moves from one part of the lake to another. Streams flowing into the lake move the water. Changes of temperature can make water near the surface sink toward the bottom. Moving water carries oxygen and nutrients to other parts of the lake.

Large lakes often have three different zones. These are the shallow-water zone, the open-water zone, and the deep-water zone. Each zone provides a different environment.

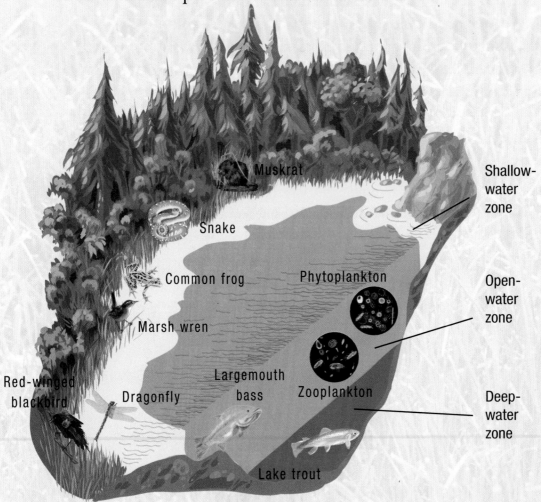

The shallow-water zone is near the shore. The water is shallow enough for sunlight to reach the lake bottom. The shallow-water zone often has rooted plants, such as water lilies, growing in the muddy bottom. Floating plants and **algae** may cover the surface of the water. Insect larvae swim around the plants and burrow into the mud. Insect larvae are food for larger animals, such as fish and frogs. Ducks, and other birds and small mammals, live in the shallow-water zone.

The open-water zone is farther out in the lake. The water is deeper. There are no rooted plants. Sunlight is bright near the surface of the open-water zone. The light is dim in the deeper water.

Two important kinds of **microscopic** organisms live in this open-water zone. **Phytoplankton** are tiny plantlike organisms. They are the "grass" of the lake environment. They are eaten by **zooplankton.** Zooplankton are microscopic animals in the lake environment. The zooplankton are food for insects and baby fish in the lake. Larger fish, such as trout and largemouth bass, live in the open-water zone. Birds, such as ducks and grebes, also live in this zone.

Phytoplankton are tiny plantlike organisms.

In big lakes, there is a deep-water zone. This zone is dark and the water is cold all the time. Water from higher levels in the lake doesn't mix with the deep zone water so there is less oxygen in the deep zone. Only animals that need little oxygen and light, live at the bottom of the lake. These animals include some insects and lake trout.

Ponds

A pond is a small, shallow body of water. Sunlight reaches to the bottom of the pond. Plants and algae may grow over the entire surface of the pond. Plants may be rooted or floating. Ponds also have large numbers of phytoplankton and zooplankton. Some animals that live in ponds are fish, birds, crayfish, frogs, snails, scuds, insects, turtles, and worms.

Lake Baikal

Lake Baikal in Russia is the world's deepest freshwater lake. It is also the largest freshwater lake by volume. Twenty percent of the fresh water on Earth is in this one lake. It is 1,637 meters (5,402 feet) deep and has a surface area of 31,468 square kilometers (12,590 square miles). The lake formed about 25 million years ago and is the oldest lake in the world. There are over 1,500 kinds of animals that live only in the Lake Baikal region.

Pollution from a nearby paper-making factory almost destroyed many of these animals in the 1950s and 1960s. Efforts to clean up the pollution have brought back much of the wildlife. However, Lake Baikal remains threatened by pollution.

Vernal Pools

A vernal pool is a shallow, temporary pond. *Vernal* means "spring." Vernal pools form when water collects in low places in the land. This happens during the rainy season or when snow melts in the spring. Vernal pools dry up during the dry season or the summer. When it is filled with water, the vernal pool is full of life. When it is dry, it looks more like a mud flat. Vernal-pool plants and animals remain **dormant** (inactive) during dry periods. When the pools fill with water again, the organisms reproduce and thrive. Salamanders, frogs, and many insects reproduce in vernal pools.

Rivers

Rivers are large, moving bodies of fresh water. They usually flow into the ocean. Rivers often flow faster near their **source** in the mountains where the land is steeper. Animals that live in the upper part of a river survive by being good swimmers or by holding tightly to rocks and twigs. Trout are strong swimmers. Insect larvae have hooks for holding on. As rivers flow toward the ocean, their currents may slow. Plants and animals in the lower parts of rivers are more like those that live in lakes. Smaller moving-water environments are creeks, brooks, and streams.

The World's Five Largest Freshwater Lakes
(based on surface area)

Lake	Location	Area in square kilometers	Area in square miles
Lake Superior	North America	82,103	32,020
Lake Victoria	Africa	69,484	27,099
Lake Huron	North America	59,600	23,244
Lake Michigan	North America	57,757	22,525
Lake Tanganyika	Africa	32,893	12,828

The World's Five Longest Rivers

River	Location	Length in kilometers	Length in miles
Nile	Africa	6,632	4,112
Amazon	South America	6,400	3,968
Mississippi/Missouri	North America	5,995	3,717
Yangtze	Asia	5,525	3,426
Orb/Irtysh	Russia	5,410	3,354

Review Questions

1. What living and nonliving factors define a lake's shallow-water zone?

2. What role do phytoplankton play in an aquatic environment?

3. How are lake and river organisms different?

INVESTIGATION 3

LS3a. Students know ecosystems can be characterized by their living and nonliving components.

What Is An Ecosystem?

An **ecosystem** is a **community** of organisms **interacting** with one another and with the nonliving environment. Your terrarium is an ecosystem. You put plants and a few small animals in a closed environment. The plants and animals are the community. Soil, air, and water are the main nonliving factors in the terrarium environment.

An aquarium is also an ecosystem. Aquariums have a community of fish, snails, and water plants. Water is the main nonliving factor in the aquarium environment.

Terrariums and aquariums are two kinds of ecosystems. And there are many more. When you go to the woods, you are visiting a natural ecosystem. Trees, grass, squirrels, birds, and insects are some of the organisms interacting with the nonliving environment in the woods ecosystem.

Ecologists are scientists who study ecosystems. They find out what kinds of plants, animals, and other organisms are living in an area. They also measure the nonliving environmental factors in the area (the temperature, soil, water, and light). Then they study how the community of organisms and the nonliving environment interact.

A woods ecosystem

Matter and Energy In an Ecosystem

Living organisms need **food** to survive. Food provides two things, **matter** and **energy.** Matter is stuff. Everything that takes up space is matter. Air, water, rock, wood, metal, machines, buildings, and organisms are all matter.

Energy makes things happen. Energy makes it possible for organisms to grow and move. Organisms use energy to sense their environment and to reproduce.

Organisms get both matter and energy from food. But the way plants get the food they need for life is very different from the way animals get their food.

Plants *make* the food they need for life. Plants get the matter and energy they need to make food from the nonliving environment.

Animals *cannot* make their own food. Animals get the food they need for life from other organisms. The way animals get food from other organisms is to eat them.

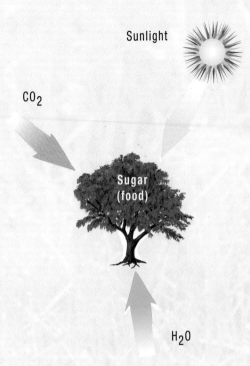

Sunlight

CO_2

Sugar (food)

H_2O

Plants use water, carbon dioxide, and sunlight to make their own food.

Energy for most ecosystems comes from the Sun. Energy from the Sun is captured by plants' green leaves. Plants use water (H_2O), carbon dioxide (CO_2), and sunlight from the nonliving environment to make sugar. Light energy is converted to chemical energy in sugar. Plants then use the energy in the sugar to live.

When animals eat plants, they use the energy from the sugar in the plants. But even though the animal gets the energy from plants, it is really energy that came from the Sun. All of the energy used by all the living organisms in an ecosystem comes from the Sun.

Review Questions

1. **How do plants and animals get the food they need to survive?**

2. **Explain how energy from the Sun helps a deer survive.**

3. **What is an ecosystem?**

LS2a. Students know plants are the primary source of matter and energy entering most food chains.

LS2b. Students know producers and consumers (herbivores, carnivores, omnivores, and decomposers) are related in food chains and food webs and may compete with each other for resources in an ecosystem.

LS2c. Students know decomposers, including many fungi, insects, and microorganisms, recycle matter from dead plants and animals.

Food Chains and Food Webs

In any ecosystem, there is a lot of eating going on. Do you remember why? Eating is the way animals get the food they need to survive. What is it about food that makes life possible? Food is a source of matter and energy. The matter in food provides the raw materials an organism needs to grow and reproduce. Energy is like fuel that makes things happen.

One way to think about ecosystems is who eats whom. When you know how an organism gets its food, you can put it into a group. Let's look at the groups.

Producers

Some organisms don't eat anything. They don't have to, because they make their own food. Organisms that make their own food are called **producers.** In terrestrial ecosystems, the most important producers are plants. Grasses, trees, and bushes are producers. In freshwater and ocean ecosystems, algae are the most important producers.

Producers use the food they make as a source of matter and energy. They never eat other organisms for matter and energy. Any organism that makes its own food is a producer.

Consumers

Organisms that eat other organisms are **consumers.**
Consumers can't make their own food. Consumers have to eat
other organisms to get their matter and energy.

Some consumers eat plants and plant parts. Deer eat grass
and leaves. Gophers eat roots. Squirrels eat nuts and berries.
Caterpillars eat leaves. Animals that eat only producers to get
their food are called **herbivores.**

Some animals don't eat plants. Snakes don't eat nuts and
berries. Hawks don't eat grass. Spiders don't eat leaves. So how
do they get their matter and energy? They eat other animals.
Snakes and hawks eat gophers and squirrels. Spiders eat insects.
Animals that eat other animals are called **carnivores.**

Some consumers, like bears, raccoons, robins, and crayfish,
eat both plants and animals. They are also called **omnivores.**

Scavengers are consumers that eat dead organisms. Some,
like vultures, eat only dead animals. Others, like isopods and
termites, eat dead leaves and wood. Coyotes, rats, ants, and
earthworms will eat just about anything that is dead.

Decomposers

There is a hidden world in every ecosystem. Millions of
insects and invisible **microorganisms** use the last bits of dead
plants and animals for food. They can be thought of as the
cleanup crew. These organisms are called **decomposers.**

Decompose means to "break into parts." Insects, such as ants,
and termites, break down dead plants and and animals into
tiny pieces. Then **fungi** and **bacteria** take over. Bacteria and
fungi break down dead plant and animal matter into simple
chemicals (nutrients). The simple chemicals are returned to
the environment. When decomposers are done with a dead
organism, the energy is all used up, and there is no longer
any food value. The simple chemicals are the raw materials
used by producers to make more food. Decomposers are the
ecosystem's matter recyclers.

Food Chains

When a spider eats a fly, the matter and energy in the fly go to the spider. This feeding relationship can be shown with an arrow. The arrow always points in the direction that the matter and energy flow.

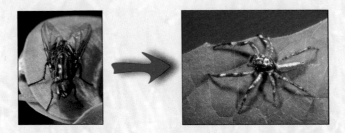

If a praying mantis eats a spider, the matter and energy in the spider go to the mantis.

It's possible in a woodland ecosystem for a jay to eat the praying mantis, a weasel to eat the jay, and a hawk to eat the weasel. Matter and energy pass from one organism to the next when they are eaten. This is called a **food chain.** And at the start of the chain is a producer. In this case, the producer is a fruit from a tree, a plum. You can draw arrows from one organism to the next to describe a food chain. The arrows show the direction of energy flow. They point from the organism that is eaten to the organism that eats it.

plum → fly → spider → mantis → jay → weasel → hawk

Another example of a food chain might start with grass, a producer. A chipmunk eats the grass seed. A hawk eats the chipmunk. Bacteria decompose any dead organisms or uneaten parts. You can always draw arrows from dead organisms to the decomposers.

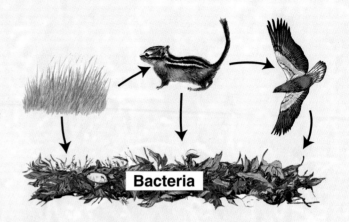

A simple food chain

Food Webs

There are many feeding relationships in an ecosystem. If you draw *all* the arrows that show who eats whom, you have a **food web,** not a food chain. The food web for a California river might look like this.

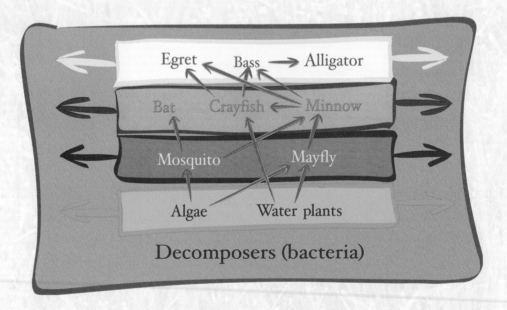

This is an example of a food web for a California river. Bacteria decompose all of the organisms when they die.

Look at the crayfish. Crayfish are eaten by both egrets and bass. If the river has a lot of crayfish, egrets and bass will both have plenty to eat. But, if there are few crayfish, the egrets and bass will have to **compete** with each other for crayfish.

The animal that can get more food is the one that is more likely to survive. In this river ecosystem, egrets and bass compete for crayfish. Are there other competitions for food in the ecosystem?

Organisms in ecosystems depend on one another for the food they need to survive. Herbivores depend on producers to make food. Carnivores depend on other animals for food. Omnivores depend on both plants and animals for food. Decomposers depend on dead organisms and waste for food. And producers depend on decomposers for raw materials to make food. In a healthy ecosystem, some organisms will be eaten, so that other organisms will survive.

Review Questions

1. **What is food? Why is it important?**

2. **Do plants need food? Why or why not?**

3. **What happens to hawks when they die?**

4. **What is the role of producers in an ecosystem?**

5. **Look at the food web for a California river on page 126. Give three examples of animals that compete for a food source.**

6. **What is the role of decomposers in an ecosystem?**

LS2a. Students know plants are the primary source of matter and energy entering most food chains.

LS2b. Students know producers and consumers (herbivores, carnivores, omnivores, and decomposers) are related in food chains and food webs and may compete with each other for resources in an ecosystem.

LS2c. Students know decomposers, including many fungi, insects, and microorganisms, recycle matter from dead plants and animals.

Monterey Bay National Marine Sanctuary

Much of the northern California coast is rocks and cliffs. The water is very cold all year. During the winter and spring, huge Pacific waves crash on the rugged shore. Can anything live in this difficult environment?

Monterey Bay

The answer is yes. The northern California coast is one of the richest ecosystems on Earth. Thousands of different kinds of organisms live and interact in the cold ocean water. This ecosystem is protected in the Monterey Bay National Marine Sanctuary. *Marine* means "ocean" or "sea." A sanctuary is a protected place. This is one place where scientists can study the interactions between ocean organisms and their environment.

The Kelp Forest

Giant kelp grows in much of the 13,730 square kilometer (5,355 square mile) sanctuary. Kelp looks like a plant, but it is actually algae. Like plants, algae make their own food. They are producers in their ecosystem.

Giant kelp are anchored to the seabed and reach clear to the ocean surface. In some places, the distance is more than 100 meters (330 feet) to the surface. This makes the kelp taller than the tallest trees. For this reason, the California marine ecosystem is often called the kelp forest.

A kelp forest

Like the rain forest, the kelp forest has a floor, an understory, and a large canopy. The canopy spreads across the water's surface. But, unlike the rain forest, most of the organisms do not live in the canopy. Most live in the understory and on the seabed. Every square centimeter of the rocky bottom has animals clinging to it. These include clams, scallops, mussels, barnacles, limpets, abalones, snails, sponges, sea urchins, sea stars, shrimp, and sea anemones. Every crack and cave shelters a fish, eel, crab, or octopus.

Garibaldi

Fish live in the understory. There are small fish such as anchovies and sardines, middle-sized fish such as sea bass, snappers, and perch, and large fish such as sharks. The California state marine fish is the bright orange garibaldi. It also lives here. Other animals found in the understory are squids, jellyfish, seals, sea lions, and gray whales.

The canopy provides shelter for a number of small animals that live on and around the kelp. These include snails, crabs, barnacles, and kelp fish. The canopy is a resting and hunting place for sea otters, sea birds, gulls, terns, ospreys, and ducks.

Where do all these animals get the food they need to survive? Like all ecosystems, the kelp forest depends on producers. The giant algae provide energy and matter to the ecosystem, but only a small amount. Microscopic phytoplankton are the most important producers in this ecosystem. These tiny producers—the grass of the sea—are eaten by zooplankton. Zooplankton are eaten by baby fish (kelp fish), clams, crabs, and thousands of other organisms. Small fish and crabs are eaten by larger fish (sea bass). The food produced by the phytoplankton eventually feeds the sea lions and sharks at the top of the food web. Marine bacteria decompose all the dead organisms in the ocean ecosystem.

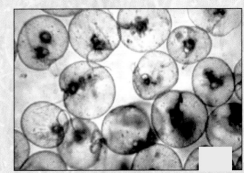
Phytoplankton

Great white shark
↑
Sea lion
↑
Sea bass
↑
Kelp fish
↑
Zooplankton
↑
Phytoplankton

Zooplankton

Competition for Resources

There is a lot of competition for phytoplankton in the marine ecosystem. The zooplankton that have the best structures for catching phytoplankton will be most successful. This is one example of competition for food.

There is competition for space. Waves and currents are very strong in the coastal environment. Many organisms must attach firmly to a solid surface or be washed away. The rocky bottom of the ocean is completely covered with organisms.

Kelp forest organisms compete for shelter. Caves, cracks, and old shells are used as hiding places. There is life and death competition for places to attach and hide.

Review Questions

1. **What do you think happens to waste and dead animals in the marine ecosystem?**

2. **What is the most important producer in both freshwater and marine ecosystems?**

3. **Identify three ways organisms compete in the marine ecosystem.**

This is a hermit crab. Hermit crabs live in empty snail shells. What kind of competition do you think they have in the ecosystem?

Summary: Aquatic Environments

Aquatic and terrestrial **ecosystems** are very different. But they are the *same* in some ways. Let's compare.

The nonliving components of the two environments are different. Aquatic ecosystems are found in water. Terrestrial ecosystems are found on land. The temperature in an aquatic ecosystem is fairly constant. The temperature in a terrestrial ecosystem can change a lot. The amount of water in an aquatic ecosystem is constant. Water in a terrestrial ecosystem can change.

The organisms are different in the two ecosystems. Most aquatic organisms can live only in water. If they are moved to a terrestrial ecosystem, they die. The same is true for terrestrial organisms moved into aquatic ecosystems.

Both ecosystems, however, are *organized* in similar ways. The organisms in aquatic and terrestrial ecosystems all need matter and energy to stay alive.

- Both ecosystems obtain **energy** from the Sun and **matter** from the environment.
- Both have **food chains** and **food webs.**
- They depend on **producers** to make **food.**
- They have **consumers** that eat the producers.
- They have **microorganisms,** such as **bacteria** and **fungi,** and other **decomposers** that break down the dead organisms and recycle the raw materials (nutrients).
- **Herbivores, carnivores, omnivores,** and scavengers live in both ecosystems.

In both ecosystems, organisms **compete** for **resources** they need to survive. Plants compete for light. Animals compete for food. Organisms need space and shelter from predators and changes in the nonliving environment. The organism that outcompetes the others is the organism that will survive.

Summary Questions

Now is a good time to review what you have recorded in your science notebook. Think about the investigations you have conducted with ecosystems.

1. **What are some of the ways all ecosystems are the same?**

2. **Where do terrestrial and aquatic ecosystems get their energy?**

3. **How do organisms in an ecosystem get the matter and energy they need to survive?**

California Science Standards

LS2a. Students know plants are the primary source of matter and energy entering most food chains.

LS2b. Students know producers and consumers (herbivores, carnivores, omnivores, and decomposers) are related in food chains and food webs and may compete with each other for resources in an ecosystem.

LS2c. Students know decomposers, including many fungi, insects, and microorganisms, recycle matter from dead plants and animals.

LS3a. Students know ecosystems can be characterized by their living and nonliving components.

LS3b. Students know that in any particular environment, some kinds of plants and animals survive well, some survive less well, and some cannot survive at all.

Vocabulary

ecosystem

energy

matter

food chain

food web

producer

food

consumer

microorganism

bacteria

fungi

decomposer

herbivore

carnivore

omnivore

compete

resources

Extensions

Math Problem of the Week

Kim's Tropical Fish

Kim wants to set up a tropical-fish aquarium. She has $20.00 to spend on the fish. The store has four types of fish for her tank. She wants at least one of each type of fish. There is no tax charged on fish. Kim wants to have $2.00 or less left after she buys all of her fish.

Type of Fish	Cost per Fish	Length of Fish
Angelfish	$ 2.98	7 cm long
Lampeye	$ 1.59	3 cm long
Mollies	$ 1.35	4 cm long
Neon tetras	$ 1.70	2 cm long

What combination of fish could she buy? How much money will she have left? Show all your work.

Kim's Aquarium Tank

Kim's parents agree to buy the aquarium tank for Kim's new fish. Kim remembers from her aquatic environments project that tropical fish need 1 liter of water for every 3 centimeters of fish length in the aquarium. What size aquarium in full liters do Kim's fish need? Show your work.

Bonus Problem

Can you find another combination of fish Kim could buy? What size tank does she need for these fish?

Home/School Connection

Look for an aquatic environment in your neighborhood. It might be a stream, lake, pond, puddle, or wet spot. Use a net to sample the environment. Record the kinds of organisms you find and organize your discoveries in a chart.

If no aquatic environment is nearby, use a local map to find out how many different kinds of aquatic environments are in your area.

INVESTIGATION 4

LS3b. Students know that in any particular environment, some kinds of plants and animals survive well, some survive less well, and some cannot survive at all.

Brine Shrimp

Brine shrimp (*Artemia*) are small crustaceans. They live only in salty aquatic environments, such as salt lakes and **brine ponds.** Unlike their relatives, the crabs and lobsters, brine shrimp cannot live in the open ocean. But brine shrimp can live in environments where most other organisms cannot.

An adult brine shrimp is about 1 centimeter (0.5 inch) long. Its partly transparent (clear) body is divided into segments. Between 11 and 19 of the brine shrimp's segments have legs. The legs are used for swimming and feeding. As it swims, it pulls nearby microscopic bits of food into its mouth.

Salt is an important nonliving factor in the environment of brine shrimp. Brine shrimp can live in a **range** of salt **concentrations.** The brine shrimp living in Mono Lake thrive when the salt concentration in the environment is 80 parts salt per 1,000 parts water. If the salt concentration drops below 60 parts salt, the brine shrimp will survive, but not as well. If the salt concentration falls below 20 parts per thousand, or goes over 100 parts per thousand, the brine shrimp will not survive.

Brine shrimp eggs can survive during long periods of dryness. They stay dormant (inactive) for up to 3 years before hatching. Live adult brine shrimp are sold as food for larger fish. Brine shrimp are sometimes sold as pets called sea monkeys.

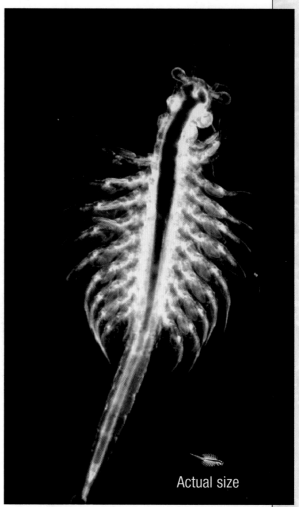

Actual size

Magnified view of a brine shrimp

LS2b. Students know producers and consumers (herbivores, carnivores, omnivores, and decomposers) are related in food chains and food webs and may compete with each other for resources in an ecosystem.

The Mono Lake Story

A view of Mono Lake

Mono Lake lies at the edge of the Great Basin in northeastern California. It is at least 760,000 years old. That makes it the oldest lake in America. Because it lies between the Sierra Nevada and the desert, Mono Lake is blistering hot in the summer and freezing cold in the winter. And Mono Lake's water is salty, even saltier than the ocean.

137

At first glance, Mono Lake looks lifeless. But it isn't. What looks like a lifeless lake is a rare and important ecosystem.

The story of the Mono Lake ecosystem starts with the lake water itself. Because it is so salty, no plants or common lake animals can live there. There are no fish, frogs, or mosquitoes in the water. But two kinds of algae thrive in the salty water. They are tiny floating algae and bottom algae. Floating algae drift around in the lake, and bottom algae grow on the lake bottom. These algae are the producers in the Mono Lake ecosystem.

Brine Shrimp

The most important animal in Mono Lake is the brine shrimp. Over the winter, the bottom of the lake is covered with billions of brine shrimp eggs. In late spring, the water starts to warm. This is when the eggs start to hatch. The tiny brine shrimp are no larger than the period at the end of this sentence. The shrimp eat the floating algae and grow. In a few weeks, they are full-sized adults. They start to reproduce. By early summer, there are trillions of brine shrimp in the lake. Mobs of several million shrimp form pink clouds all over the lake.

Many birds **migrate** from winter feeding grounds to spring nesting grounds. Mono Lake plays an important role in the survival of several kinds of birds. About 50,000 California gulls migrate from the ocean to Mono Lake to reproduce. The gulls make nests on the two islands in Mono Lake and feed on the brine shrimp. When their eggs hatch, the gull parents catch brine shrimp to feed their chicks. By the middle of the summer, the chicks can fly. They follow their parents over the mountains to the ocean.

Pink clouds of brine shrimp in Mono Lake

Mono Lake in the summer

California gulls feeding chicks

But there is still more happening at Mono Lake. Small shorebirds called phalaropes and waterbirds called eared grebes also stop at Mono Lake to eat and rest. They reproduce in Canada and then fly south for the winter. Without Mono Lake as a place to rest and feed, they would not be able to finish their migration.

An amazing 150,000 phalaropes and 1–2 million grebes come to Mono Lake during the summer. By midsummer the lake is clear. The brine shrimp have eaten most of the algae. There are trillions of shrimp in the lake. The phalaropes and grebes eat and eat and eat. By the time the birds are ready to continue their migration, only a few billion brine shrimp are left in the lake.

As the water cools in the fall, the last brine shrimp females lay eggs. These eggs don't hatch. They settle to the bottom of the lake. With the brine shrimp gone for the time being, the floating algae reproduce in huge numbers. The eggs lay dormant until the next spring. When the water warms up again, the eggs hatch. The new shrimp begin eating the algae, and the whole cycle starts again.

Brine Flies

While the brine shrimp are eating the floating algae, the larvae of the brine fly are eating the bottom algae. When the larvae are full grown, they come to the lake's surface and pupate. In a few days, the pupae open and the adult flies come out. There are billions of them on the shore of Mono Lake.

Brine flies along the water's edge

Close-up of brine flies

Today the brine flies are another food source for the phalaropes, gulls, and grebes. In the past, brine flies were food for the native people living in the Mono Basin. The word *mono* may be a Native American word that means "fly eater." The Native American people who lived in the basin would gather millions of the pupae, dry them in the sunshine, and store them for winter food. The pupae had a lot of protein and fat, and were easy to harvest.

Humans In the Mono Lake Ecosystem

For thousands of years, Mono Lake was where the California gulls came to reproduce. In 1941, things began to change.

The Los Angeles Department of Water and Power began taking water from four of the seven streams that flow into Mono Lake. The water was sent 560 kilometers (347 miles) away for the people in Los Angeles. The result was an ecological disaster for Mono Lake. The lake shrank to half its size. The salt concentration in the lake water doubled.

In 1982, the salt concentration in Mono Lake was making it hard for algae and brine flies to survive. The brine shrimp were in trouble, too. These changes affected the California gulls. They didn't have as much food to eat.

The lower water level caused a land bridge between shore and one of the California gull nesting islands. Foxes and coyotes could walk to the island and eat the eggs and chicks. Because of the predators and lack of food, the California gulls did not raise any chicks that year.

Mono Lake Makes a Comeback

In 1978, a young man named David Gaines (1947–1988) became concerned about the poor environmental condition of Mono Lake. He formed an action group called the Mono Lake Committee. Under his leadership, the committee worked with government agencies, environmental groups, and the Los Angeles water department to solve the problem.

In 1994, a decision was finally reached. Less water would go to Los Angeles. This would allow the water level in Mono Lake to slowly rise.

David Gaines

Today the water in the lake has returned to a good level. The salt concentration has gone down. The land bridge to the island is again underwater. The brine shrimp and brine flies are thriving. The California gulls are raising chicks. The Mono Lake story shows that people can take positive action to restore the environment and save important ecosystems.

Review Questions

1. **What is the main environmental factor that affects the well-being of the Mono Lake ecosystem? Explain your answer.**

2. **Why did the California gull chicks not survive at Mono Lake in 1982?**

3. **Describe two kinds of competition in the Mono Lake ecosystem.**

4. **Do you think the migrating birds are part of the Mono Lake ecosystem? Explain your answer.**

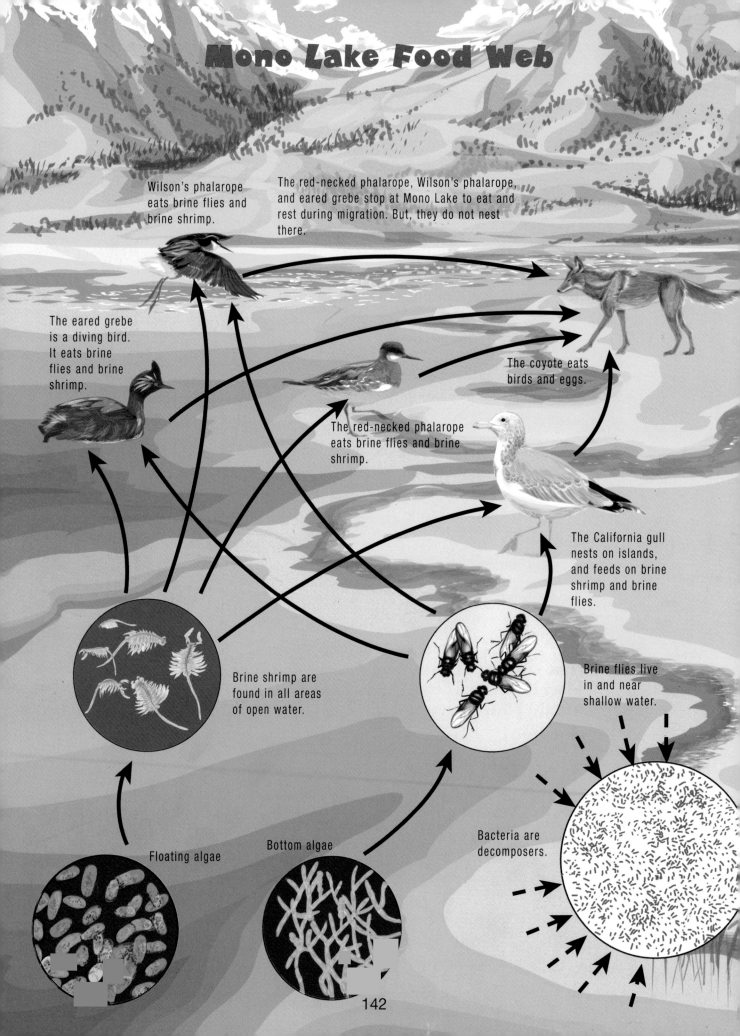

Mono Lake Food Web

Wilson's phalarope eats brine flies and brine shrimp.

The red-necked phalarope, Wilson's phalarope, and eared grebe stop at Mono Lake to eat and rest during migration. But, they do not nest there.

The eared grebe is a diving bird. It eats brine flies and brine shrimp.

The coyote eats birds and eggs.

The red-necked phalarope eats brine flies and brine shrimp.

The California gull nests on islands, and feeds on brine shrimp and brine flies.

Brine shrimp are found in all areas of open water.

Brine flies live in and near shallow water.

Floating algae

Bottom algae

Bacteria are decomposers.

LS2c. Students know decomposers, including many fungi, insects, and microorganisms, recycle matter from dead plants and animals.

LS3d. Students know that most microorganisms do not cause disease and that many are beneficial.

Microorganisms

What do you think a microorganism might be? *Micro* means "very small." *Organism* means "a living thing." A microorganism is a living organism that is so small that you can't see it with your bare eyes.

What do you think of when you hear the word *bacteria* or *fungi*? Getting sick and moldy bread? Bacteria can cause **disease,** and fungi can make bread moldy. But there is much more to the story. Bacteria and fungi are kinds of microorganisms. Like all microorganisms, bacteria and fungi are alive.

Bacteria and Fungi

Bacteria are the smallest organisms in the world. They are found in all environments. Bacteria play a very important role in every ecosystem. They act as the cleanup crew. Bacteria decompose dead matter and waste. They use the last of the energy in the dead matter, and return raw materials to the environment. Some bacteria can cause disease, but most bacteria have important roles in ecosystems.

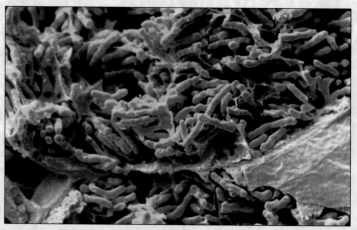
Soil bacteria

Fungi are important decomposers, too. They come in different shapes, sizes, and types. We know them as molds, mildew, and mushrooms. Like bacteria, fungi can live everywhere. They can live in both terrestrial and aquatic ecosystems. They are in the soil, in your house, on plants and animals, and even on you. A spoonful of soil might contain 120,000 fungi. Some are harmful to living plants and animals. But most fungi are important in recycling dead matter for raw materials in the environment.

Algae

Algae are microorganisms that play an important role in aquatic ecosystems. Algae produce most of the food in freshwater and marine ecosystems. They use water and carbon dioxide and sunlight to make their own food, just like plants. Algae are the food source for many kinds of crustaceans, insects, fish, and worms. When you set up your goldfish aquarium, you may have seen algae growing. Did the water turn green? Did a green layer form on the sides of the aquarium? If so, then you saw algae.

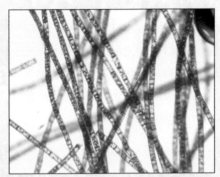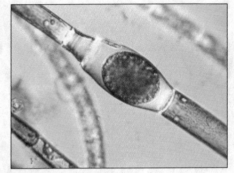

A type of freshwater algae called Oedogonium

But wait! If algae are microorganisms, how can you see them? When a few algae are in your aquarium, you won't see them because they are so small. But they start to reproduce. And after a week or two, the population of algae will be in the billions! That's what you see. Any one of those microorganisms by itself is much too small to see. You need a microscope to see just one. But huge numbers of them can be seen as green water or a green layer.

What happens to all that algae? In Mono Lake, it is food for the brine shrimp and brine flies. In a freshwater lake, insects and fish eat the algae. In the ocean, algae are food for baby clams, barnacles, corals, and thousands of baby fish, crabs, and snails.

Microorganisms and Humans

Did you know that bacteria, fungi, and algae are also found in many foods that *you* eat? Bacteria turn milk into cheese and yogurt. Both bacteria and fungi help give many cheeses their flavor. **Yeast** is a type of fungus that is used to make bread. And many kinds of algae are found in drinks, medicines, and even ice cream.

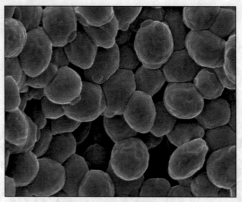
Baker's yeast cells

Not only are bacteria found in foods, they're also found *on* you and *in* you. Termites' guts contain a microorganism that helps decompose the wood they eat. And inside you, microorganisms decompose food you eat. This is part of **digestion.** Without microorganisms, you wouldn't be able to eat all the foods you like.

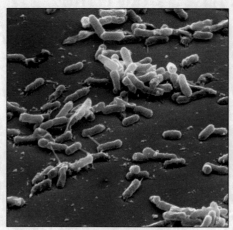
Intestinal bacteria

Sometimes dangerous bacteria get in your body. They can attack and decompose cells. This is called a bacterial infection. But bacteria that cause diseases are rare. Most of the thousands of different kinds of bacteria are good for the environment in which they live. They are not dangerous for humans.

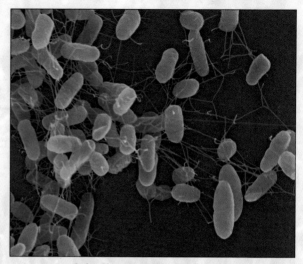

A food-poisoning bacterium
Salmonella enteritidis

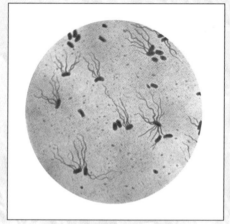

The typhoid fever bacterium
Salmonella typhi

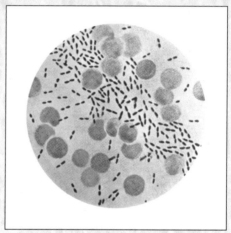

A pneumonia causing bacterium
Streptococcus pneumoniae

Review Questions

1. **Are bacteria good organisms or bad organisms? Explain your answer.**

2. **What kinds of microorganisms are producers?**

3. **In what kinds of ecosystems are microorganisms the most important producers?**

Summary: Brine Shrimp Hatching

Mono Lake is a very salty ecosystem. Most aquatic organisms cannot survive in Mono Lake because of the high salt **concentration.** But a few kinds of algae thrive in the lake. These algae are the producers that support the Mono Lake ecosystem.

One kind of alga is small and lives its life floating around in the lake. One individual alga is too small to see. That makes it a microorganism. But when countless billions of algae fill the lake, you can see them. The water turns green.

Like all ecosystems, Mono Lake has consumers. The two most important consumers are the brine shrimp and the brine flies. Millions of migrating birds stop at Mono Lake every year. The birds eat the brine shrimp and brine flies. The migrating birds would not survive if shrimp and flies were not in Mono Lake.

Bacteria are the decomposers in Mono Lake. These microorganisms break down the dead algae, brine shrimp, brine flies, birds, and waste into simple chemicals. The simple chemicals are recycled back into the ecosystem. These chemicals are the raw materials used by algae to make food the next year. Bacteria are an important part of the Mono Lake ecosystem.

A simple Mono Lake food web looks like this.

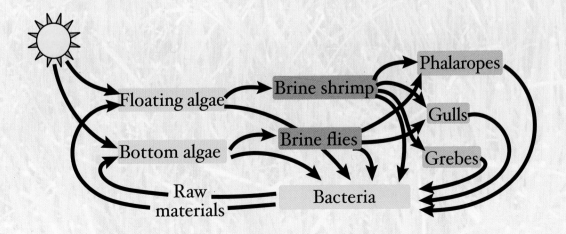

The microorganisms in Mono Lake are very important to the ecosystem. Most microorganisms do not cause **disease.** As in the case of the algae and bacteria in Mono Lake, most are beneficial.

Summary Questions

Now is a good time to review what you have recorded in your science notebook. Think about the investigations you have conducted with brine shrimp.

1. Are the algae floating in Mono Lake alive or not? Explain your answer.

2. Describe one food chain in the Mono Lake ecosystem.

3. What microorganisms live in Mono Lake? Are these microorganisms harmful or helpful to the ecosystem? Why do you think so?

California Science Standards

LS2b. Students know producers and consumers (herbivores, carnivores, omnivores, and decomposers) are related in food chains and food webs and may compete with each other for resources in an ecosystem.

LS2c. Students know decomposers, including many fungi, insects, and microorganisms, recycle matter from dead plants and animals.

LS3b. Students know that in any particular environment, some kinds of plants and animals survive well, some survive less well, and some cannot survive at all.

LS3d. Students know that most microorganisms do not cause disease and that many are beneficial.

Vocabulary

concentration

disease

Extensions

Math Problem of the Week

Kevin's Experiment. Kevin wants to set up a brine shrimp experiment to find out the best salt concentration to hatch shrimp. He has six containers that each hold 0.75 liter of water. He will use a spoonful of brine shrimp per container. Kevin starts with one-eighth of a spoon of salt for the first container.

Amount of Salt Used
Container 1   1/8 spoon of salt
Container 2   Twice as much salt as he put in Container 1
Container 3   Twice as much salt as he put in Container 2
Container 4   Twice as much salt as he put in Container 3
Container 5   Twice as much salt as he put in Container 4
Container 6   Twice as much salt as he put in Container 5

How much salt did Kevin need for all six containers? Show all of your work. Use drawings, tables, and/or charts to help you.

Maria's Experiment. Maria set up a series of six brine shrimp experiments. She wanted to find out the best salt concentration for hatching shrimp. Maria put 1 liter of water and 1 little spoonful of brine shrimp eggs in each of six containers. Then she added a different amount of salt to each container using the following pattern:

Amount of Salt Used
Container 1   8 spoons of salt
Container 2   Half as much salt as she put in Container 1
Container 3   Half as much salt as she put in Container 2
Container 4   Half as much salt as she put in Container 3
Container 5   Half as much salt as she put in Container 4
Container 6   Half as much salt as she put in Container 5

How much salt did Maria need for all six containers? Show all of your work. Use drawings, tables, and/or charts to help you.

Home/School Connection

Raise sea monkeys (brine shrimp) at home with your family. Your teacher will provide you with the eggs to get started.

LS3a. Students know ecosystems can be characterized by their living and nonliving components.

LS3b. Students know that in any particular environment, some kinds of plants and animals survive well, some survive less well, and some cannot survive at all.

Water Pollution: The Lake Erie Story

Lake Erie is one of the five Great Lakes on the border between the United States and Canada. The other four lakes are Lake Superior, Lake Michigan, Lake Huron, and Lake Ontario. Together they form the largest freshwater body in the world. In fact, 95 percent of our nation's fresh water is in the Great Lakes.

Humans caused an ecological problem in Lake Erie. For years, sewage, farm runoff, and industrial waste were dumped and washed into Lake Erie. By the 1960s, the lake had become very **polluted.** The environment had changed. Too much algae grew in the water. The amount of oxygen in the lake dropped. This made it difficult for fish to survive. There were large areas of the lake bottom where life did not exist. The lake's aquatic organisms were dying. The ecosystem was in serious trouble.

In the 1970s, people started to save Lake Erie. The United States and Canada cleaned it up. Together the two countries spent millions of dollars to develop a plan to save Lake Erie. Here is part of the plan.

- Build new and better sewage treatment plants.
- Reduce the use of detergents containing phosphates. Phosphates act as **fertilizer** for algae.
- Manage the use of fertilizers and **pesticides** on farms.
- Stop industries from dumping waste into the lake.

The efforts of both governments and the people living and working around Lake Erie paid off. The lake began to recover. After many years, the lake is much safer and healthier. The lake environment now supports many fish and other animals.

Lake Erie still has problems. More than 300 humanmade chemicals are still found in Lake Erie. Some are poisonous. The United States and Canada continue to study ways to improve the water quality. Much has been done to help this important aquatic ecosystem. But the fight to save Lake Erie is not over.

Sources of Water Pollution

■ **Farming** Pesticides are poisons used to kill pests on crops. Fertilizers are used to make crops grow better. When farmers use too much pesticide and fertilizer, the extra can wash into rivers and lakes. Fertilizers cause too much growth of aquatic plants and algae. This upsets the balance in aquatic ecosystems. Pesticides kill plants and animals in the water.

■ **Sewage** Human sewage and waste from farm animals can also get into aquatic systems. These act like fertilizers, causing aquatic plants and algae to grow. Sewage can also carry microorganisms that cause diseases in humans.

■ **Sediment** **Runoff** is water that flows over the land and then into large bodies of water. Runoff can carry soil and chemicals from mines, fields, forests, and cities. These materials settle to the bottom of lakes as **sediments.** Sediments can bury aquatic plants and animals. This burial can damage the environment and the organisms that live there.

■ **Acids** Industrial gases from smokestacks enter the air. The gases form acid in clouds. Acid rain falls from these clouds and changes the acid levels in aquatic ecosystems. Many aquatic plants and animals are sensitive to acid. When the acid level changes, some organisms continue to survive, some survive poorly, and some cannot survive at all.

■ **Petroleum** Oil spills and runoff from city streets can put oil and other **petroleum** products into lakes. Oil is harmful to animals that live on the lake surface, like waterbirds. It also harms organisms that live on the lakeshore, like snails, insects, and crayfish.

Review Questions

1. **What organism causes most of the pollution in Lake Erie? Give examples of why you think so.**

2. **What is the effect of water pollution on an aquatic ecosystem like Lake Erie?**

LS3a. Students know ecosystems can be characterized by their living and nonliving components.

LS3b. Students know that in any particular environment, some kinds of plants and animals survive well, some survive less well, and some cannot survive at all.

What Happens When Ecosystems Change?

Two things define an ecosystem. The first is the organisms. The second is the nonliving environment. The desert ecosystem of southern California is partly defined by its common organisms. Cacti, lizards, and coyotes live in the desert. So do spiders, insects, birds, scorpions, and snakes. The environment is hot and dry most of the time. The desert ecosystem thrives with these organisms and environmental conditions.

A desert ecosystem

The kelp forest ecosystem of northern California is very different. The common organisms include several kinds of kelp, fish, and sea urchins. Clams, seals, sharks, and gulls are also part of this ecosystem. The environment is cold, wet, and often overcast. The kelp forest ecosystem thrives with these organisms and environmental conditions.

A California kelp forest ecosystem

Moving desert organisms to the ocean would be silly. Cacti and snakes from the desert would not survive in the coastal kelp forest. The environment is too different. Organisms have needs. Those needs are met only by the environment in which the organisms live. But what happens when the environment changes a little bit? Are organisms affected?

We can look at the Colorado River as an example. Before 1963, the river ran free through the Grand Canyon. Each spring the melting snow upstream caused a flood in the river. The flood of cold water roared through the riverbed. It washed away the sandy beaches. It cleared out plants growing on the banks of the river.

During the summer, the river slowed. Sand settled on the edges of the river. The water warmed up. Plants began to grow on the new sandy beaches. The organisms in the river thrived in this environment.

The Colorado River ecosystem

In 1963, the Glen Canyon Dam was completed. The dam stops the flow of floodwater each spring. The water is released at the bottom of the dam at a steady rate. There are no more floods. The water flowing in the river is cold all year long.

This change in the environment was small. But it affected the balance of organisms in the ecosystem.

Trout need cold water to thrive. After the dam was completed, the trout population grew

The Glen Canyon Dam changed the Colorado River ecosystem.

because the water was cold all year. The trout became predators on the chub fish living in the river. The chub population got smaller because more trout were in the river.

Trout have a **range of tolerance** for temperature. If the water gets warmer than they can tolerate, or colder than they can tolerate, they will not survive. Before the dam was built, the warmer summer water was within the range of tolerance for trout, so they survived OK. After the dam was built, the colder water was the **optimum** (best) temperature for trout. As a result, the trout thrived and ate more of the chub.

The willows and other plants that grew on the sandy beaches were no longer washed away in the spring floods. More plants grew in the changed environment. The plants stopped the sand from moving in the riverbed. As a result, the shallow water where the baby chubs and river snails grew up disappeared. So the chub and snail populations became smaller.

This Colorado River story shows how living and nonliving environmental factors affect organisms. The environment controls which organisms will thrive, survive, and die. Small changes in temperature, water flow, or population size can change the balance of an ecosystem. The change favors some organisms and makes it harder for others.

Review Questions

1. **How did the change of water temperature affect the chub population? Why?**

2. **What living and nonliving factors describe an ecosystem?**

3. **Give examples of an organism that can survive well in the desert ecosystem, one that can survive less well, and one that cannot survive at all.**

Edward Osbourne Wilson

As a child, Edward O. Wilson (1929–) loved nature. He loved exploring in the Alabama woods and nearby streams. When he was 9 years old, he read an article about ants. Their interesting behavior and the way they worked together fascinated him. Those Alabama ants started young Wilson's career as a scientist. When he was only 13 years old, he discovered the first fire ants in the United States.

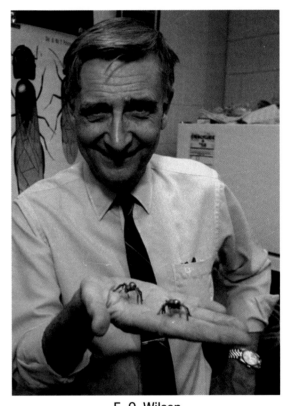
E. O. Wilson

Wilson had a hard time with math and some trouble reading. But this did not stop him from studying science. He studied biology at the University of Alabama and Harvard University. Later he became a professor at Harvard.

Wilson continued to study ants. In 1975, he wrote a book about the social behavior of ants. He described how ants and other animals communicate using chemicals called pheromones. In the book, he also compared the organization of ant colonies to human societies.

In 1992, Wilson wrote a book called *The Diversity of Life*. He wrote that human activities were destroying organisms worldwide. Wilson predicted that millions of kinds of plants and animals would become extinct by the middle of the 21st century. Since then Wilson has been trying to find ways that humans can save the world's ecosystems.

Rachel Carson

n 1962, Rachel Carson's (1907–1964) book called *Silent Spring* was published. Many people think it is the most important book about ecology ever written. It changed how Americans think about their place in nature.

Carson studied marine biology in college. In 1936, the U.S. Bureau of Fisheries hired her. She was the first woman biologist ever hired by the bureau. During the 1940s and 1950s, she studied and wrote about life in the sea. She also started to see some disturbing things happening in the environment. Animals were dying. She figured out that the cause was pesticides.

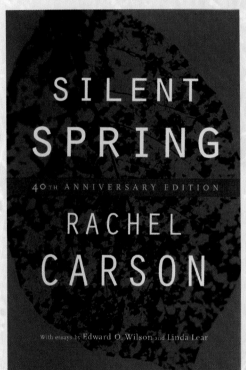

Pesticides developed in the 1940s were used widely to kill mosquitoes, fruit flies, cabbage worms, and lots of other pests. Carson discovered that the poisons also killed all the other insects in the area where the pesticide was sprayed. The poison killed everything.

When pesticide spray drifted over a friend's bird sanctuary, the birds died. Carson was alarmed. She imagined a spring when no birds returned to the woods near her home. In 1957, she started writing a book. The horrible thought of spring without the music of singing birds became the name for her book, *Silent Spring.*

The book got a lot of attention. The companies that made the pesticides tried to get the book banned. They attacked Carson and her scientific conclusions. She fought back and continued to present her evidence. Soon people started to listen, including President John F. Kennedy. President Kennedy ordered studies of a pesticide called DDT to see if Carson's ideas were right.

Rachel Carson

Carson warned us of a danger to Earth's ecosystems. It was up to others, including many environmental groups, to act on her warning. As a result of *Silent Spring*, DDT was banned in 1972. But Carson never saw the day. In 1964, she lost her battle with cancer.

Carson is best remembered for making people aware of the dangers of pesticides. People started thinking about what happens to plants and animals when we change the environment either by accident or on purpose.

Tyrone B. Hayes

Tyrone B. Hayes (1967–) is a biology professor at the University of California at Berkeley. He studies frogs. The first frogs he saw were in a swamp near his home in South Carolina. Now Hayes studies frogs in Africa and North America.

Tyrone Hayes

Hayes found something strange happening to some of the frogs he studied. Frogs living in the wild were going through sex changes. The "male" frogs were making eggs just like the females.

Hayes and his team studied the frogs' environment. They found small amounts of a common **herbicide** in the water. An herbicide is a chemical used to kill plants. Hayes did more tests in the lab. The tests showed that the herbicide was causing the changes in the frogs.

The companies that make the herbicide challenged the research. But Hayes believes his science is correct. He continues to speak out about what he finds.

Wangari Muta Maathai

Wangari Muta Maathai (1940–) was born in Nyeri, a town in Kenya, Africa. Unlike most of the young women in her country, Maathai was able to go to college. She went to college in Kansas, Pennsylvania, and in Nairobi. She was the first woman from eastern Africa to receive a doctorate degree.

In 1977, Maathai founded the Green Belt Movement. The group is mostly women. Their main activity is planting trees to replace those cut down for firewood. They have planted more than 30 million trees! But some people didn't understand the value of planting trees. They didn't see the good Maathai was doing for the environment. Even though people tried to stop her, she did what was right for the environment and for the people of Kenya.

Wangari Muta Maathai

Maathai was elected to the Kenyan Parliament in 2002. She was named deputy minister of Kenyan Natural Resources and Wildlife in 2003. In 2004, Maathai received the Nobel Peace Prize for her many years of promoting peace and good living conditions in Africa.

Summary: Range of Tolerance

Ecosystems are defined by the nonliving factors of the environment and the organisms living there. Water is a nonliving factor. Every ecosystem must have water. But the amount of water in an ecosystem can be different. Lake and ocean ecosystems thrive underwater. Rain forest ecosystems thrive with a lot of water. Desert ecosystems thrive with very little water.

A chaparral ecosystem

Chaparral ecosystems are found in the dry hills of California. Chaparral is not quite as dry as desert. But plants and animals living there must survive long summers and falls without rain. The plants are tough and brushy with long roots. Many of the animals burrow deeply into the rocky soil.

Another nonliving factor in chaparral ecosystems is fire. Wildfires leave the land's surface black and lifeless. Before long, life returns. Animals that hide deep in their burrows come back to the surface after the fire passes. The roots of chaparral plants are still alive. As soon as the rains come, new branches and leaves sprout. The ashes from the burned plants provide nutrients for the new plants to grow and thrive. The chaparral ecosystem can survive well even when wildfire burns it to the ground.

Chaparral after a fire

Chaparral new growth

The chaparral ecosystem has plants and animals that can thrive even when there are fires. The plants and animals that live here have a high **range of tolerance** for heat and fire. Plants and animals whose **optimum** environment is a forest ecosystem might survive in the chaparral ecosystem, but not nearly as well. They do not have as much tolerance for heat and fire. Plants and animals that live in rain forests would die in the chaparral ecosystem. They have no tolerance for heat and fire.

Summary Questions

Now is a good time to review what you have recorded in your science notebook. Think about the investigations you have conducted with range of tolerance.

1. **All plants need water. For a plant, what is meant by optimum conditions for water? For a plant, what is meant by range of tolerance for water?**

2. **Say someone told you she saw frogs, dragonflies, catfish, and crayfish. What kind of ecosystem did she see? Why do you think so?**

California Science Standards

LS3a. Students know ecosystems can be characterized by their living and nonliving components.

LS3b. Students know that in any particular environment, some kinds of plants and animals survive well, some survive less well, and some cannot survive at all.

Vocabulary

range of tolerance

optimum

Extensions

Math Problem of the Week

Bert's Spring Box

Bert needs water for his cabbage garden. On a hillside above the garden, he built a spring box to get underground water. Bert put a pipe from the box to his garden.

The spring box needs to fill with water to the top of the box before the water will flow into the garden.

Bert saw that the water level came up 5 centimeters in the spring box each night and then went down 3 centimeters during the day.

Bert's spring box is 20 centimeters from the bottom of the box to the top where pipe is attached.

On what day or night will water first flow into Bert's cabbage garden?

Show all your work. You can use drawings, a chart, or a number line to help you.

Learning More about Environments

Terrestrial Environments

Make a Terrarium of Local Organisms

Find local organisms, like worms, snails, slugs, and beetles, around school or in your neighborhood. Don't use animals that sting or bite (ants, bees, centipedes). Plan what kinds of materials and environmental conditions they will need.

To make sure the animals stay healthy, keep them in the classroom for only a couple of weeks. Then return them to their natural environments.

Make Terrariums from Around the World

Find clear and colorless containers for terrariums. Two-liter soda bottles are good for small terrariums. Large spring-water containers are good for large terrariums.

Did you once live in a place where the environmental conditions are different from those around your school? Try to design a terrarium that models that environment. Locate plants that are like those in that environment. Label the terrarium for the place it represents.

Sample Terrestrial Environments

Use a sweep net (a butterfly net) to sample the organisms in different terrestrial environments (grassy area, weedy area, brush area). Use the net like a broom to sweep back and forth just at the tops of plants. Record on a chart the kinds and numbers of organisms found in each environment. Insect field guides can help identify the organisms.

Investigate Beetle Metamorphosis

Study the conditions most favorable to mealworm metamorphosis. Think about the nonliving factors such as temperature, moisture, and light.

Visit a Nursery or Botanical Garden

Visit a local nursery or botanical garden. Find out about cold- and heat-tolerant plants or sun- and shade-tolerant plants.

Aquatic Environments

Design and Build a Large Aquarium

Plan and make a large aquarium for your class. It can become a permanent part of the classroom. Decide how to share the responsibilities for caring for the aquatic ecosystem.

Add Other Fish

Introduce new fish into the aquariums. Observe which parts of the environment the new fish prefer. Observe and record interactions between the different kinds of fish. (Be aware that goldfish will eat smaller fish.) Ask at a local aquarium store about fish that will be suitable to add to a goldfish aquarium.

Observe the Movement of Snails

Snails are always on the move. Trace the path of a snail for a period of time. Design a method for recording its travels.

Monitor the Growth of Duckweed

Duckweed can quickly take over the surface of an aquarium. Find out how this plant grows. Put one or two plants in a cup of water and observe them over time.

Observe Adult Brine Shrimp

Make a brine shrimp environment using the recipe below. Buy live adult brine shrimp at a pet store. They are food for tropical fish. Transfer them to your environment. Observe their structures and behaviors.

Recipe for brine shrimp environment (metric)

1 liter	Pure water (bottled drinking water is good)
10 ml	Rock salt
5 ml	Epsom salts
2 ml	Baking soda

Recipe for brine shrimp environment (English)

1	qt.	Pure water (bottled drinking water is good)
6	tb.	Rock salt
1	tsp.	Epsom salts
1/2 tsp.		Baking soda

Grow Brine Shrimp to Adults

Grow brine shrimp from eggs to adults in one of the 6-liter basins. Use the recipe above to prepare the environment. Feed the brine shrimp with drops of yeast mixture (see below). A large group of brine shrimp (1 minispoon of eggs) might take 10 drops every few days. A small group of brine shrimp (100–200 adults) will need only 3–4 drops. Do not overfeed. With luck you should be able to maintain brine shrimp for a long time. You can observe swimming, mating, life cycle, and response to light.

Yeast Mixture

Put 0.5 milliliter (1/8 teaspoon) of dry baker's yeast in 30 milliliters (1 ounce) of pure water. Stir and shake the mixture until the yeast makes the water cloudy. Put it in a dropper bottle. Keep the yeast mixture in a refrigerator.

Investigate Brine Shrimp and Light

Design an experiment to find out how brine shrimp respond to the environmental factor of light.

List Wet and Dry Words

Work in your group to make lists of words that describe degrees of wetness. Then put the words in order from driest to wettest.

Use Water Gauges

Visit a nursery to see what kinds of devices are available to monitor soil moisture in houseplants. Some are simple and inexpensive. Bring one to class and use it to monitor soil moisture in a classroom plant.

Environmental Issues

Keep an Environmental-News Bulletin Board

Find newspaper articles about environmental factors and their influence on organisms. Make a bulletin board of articles that discuss issues in California. Prepare a short report on one of the issues.

Investigate Effects of Gray Water

Reusing water conserves water. Find out what happens to plants when kitchen-sink gray water is the water source. Use different concentrations of the gray water.

Research Drought Areas

Research the impact of drought around the world, the process of land conversion to desert, and the loss of food production.

Research Salt on Roads

In many areas of the country, people spread salt on icy roads to speed up melting. Find out if salt is used in the icy parts of California.

Simulate Acid Rain

Design and conduct an experiment to investigate the effect of acid rain on plants. Use different concentrations of vinegar.

Life Sciences Glossary

Adult   The last stage in a life cycle when the organism is mature and can reproduce.

Algae   A large group of water organisms.

Amphibian   An organism, such as a spadefoot toad, that reproduces in water.

Antenna (pl. antennae)   A feeler on the head of an isopod or insect.

Bacteria   Microorganisms that act as decomposers.

Behavior   The actions or responses of organisms to something in their environment.

Brine pond   A saltwater environment where brine shrimp live.

Burrow   A hole or tunnel dug by a small animal.

Canopy   The highest layer in the rain forest where there is a lot of sunlight.

Carnivore   An animal that eats other animals.

Community   The plants and animals in an ecosystem.

Compete   To rely on or need the same resource as another organism.

Competition   A demand for resources, such as food or water or space, by two or more organisms.

Complete metamorphosis   The cycle of growth changes for an insect. The stages include egg, larva, pupa, and adult.

Component   A part of something.

Concentration   The amount of a substance, such as salt, in an amount of another substance, such as water.

Consumer   An organism that cannot make its own food. Consumers eat other organisms.

Crustacean An animal with a shell, jaw, and two pairs of antennae. Most crustaceans live in water. Crabs, lobsters, shrimp, and isopods are examples of crustaceans.

Decomposer An organism that breaks down plant and animal material into simple chemicals. The chemicals can then be reused in the ecosystem.

Desert A major terrestrial environment on Earth that receives less than 25 centimeters (10 inches) of rain each year.

Digestion The process of reducing food into nutrients that can be absorbed by the body.

Disease A sickness.

Dormant An organism in an inactive or in a resting state, such as a dormant seed or egg.

Ecologist A scientist who studies ecosystems.

Ecosystem A community of organisms interacting with each other and with the nonliving environment.

Egg The first stage of an animal's life cycle.

Energy What makes organisms grow and move.

Entomologist A biologist who studies insects.

Environment Everything that surrounds and influences an organism.

Environmental factor One part of the environment. An environmental factor can be nonliving, such as water, light, and temperature. It can be living, such as plants and animals.

Evaporate To dry up and go into the air.

Fertile The condition of being able to support growth and development. Soil can be fertile if it will support the growth of plants.

Fertilizer Any natural or synthetic material used in soil to help plants grow.

Food   A form of chemical energy that organisms need to survive. Plants make their own food. Animals eat other organisms for food.

Food chain   A description of the feeding sequence of one set of organisms in an ecosystem, such as grass seeds, chipmunk, and hawk. Arrows point in the direction of the flow of energy from one organism to another.

Food web   A description of the feeding relationships between all of the organisms in an ecosystem. Arrows show the flow of energy from one organism to another.

Forest floor   The bottom layer of the rain forest where there is very little light.

Function   The purpose or use of something, such as the function of a body part.

Fungus (pl. fungi)   An organism that lacks chlorophyll and absorbs nutrients from dead or living organisms. Mushrooms and yeast are examples of fungi.

Gill   A breathing structure of an animal that lives in water or very moist environments.

Grassland   A major terrestrial environment on Earth where the land is flat or hilly, such as a prairie.

Herbicide   A chemical used to kill plants.

Herbivore   An animal that eats plants.

Insect   An animal that has six legs, a head, a thorax, and an abdomen.

Interact   To act upon one another.

Isopod   A small crustacean with 14 legs that all function the same.

Larva (pl. larvae)   The wormlike early stage in the life cycle of an insect.

Living   The condition of being alive.

Matter   Anything that takes up space.

Mealworm   The larva of a beetle.

Microorganism   A microscopic organism, such as bacteria and algae.

Microscopic   Too small to be seen with your bare eyes.

Migrate   To move from one area to another.

Nocturnal   To be active at night.

Nonliving   Something that has never been alive, or things that were once alive and are no longer alive.

Nutrient   A substance or raw material needed for the maintenance, growth, and development of an organism.

Omnivore   An animal that eats both plants and other animals.

Optimum   The best condition that is favorable to growth, development, and reproduction of an organism.

Organism   Any living thing, including all plants and animals.

Parasite   An organism that lives on or in another living organism.

Pesticide   A chemical developed to kill animals that are in some way harmful to humans.

Petroleum   A dark oil.

Phytoplankton   Microscopic plantlike organisms in aquatic environments that produce their own food. Zooplankton eat phytoplankton.

Pill bug   An isopod that can roll up into a ball.

Pollination   The moving of pollen to the female part of a flower.

Pollute   To make an environment unsuitable for organisms because of substances introduced into air, water, or soil.

Predator   An animal that hunts other animals for food.

Producer   An organism, such as a plant or alga, that makes its own food.

Pupa (pl. pupae)   The stage of an animal's life cycle between the larva and the adult stages.

Range   An amount of variation or difference.

Range of tolerance   The varying conditions of one environmental factor in which an organism can survive.

Recycle   To use again.

Reproduce   To create offspring.

Resource   A material available for use by organisms. Food, water, air, shelter, space, or nutrients are examples of resources.

Runoff   Water that flows over the land and into bodies of water.

Scavenger   An animal that eats dead organisms.

Sediment   Tiny bits of rock, shell, dead plants, or other material that settle out of a fluid.

Seed dispersal   The movement of seeds away from the parent plant.

Shelter   A home or place that gives protection to organisms.

Source   The beginning of something, such as where a river starts.

Sow bug   An isopod that is flat, has long antennae, and can't roll up into a ball.

Sprout   To start to grow.

Structure   A physical feature or part of an organism.

Survive   To remain alive.

Taiga   A major terrestrial environment on Earth with fir and spruce trees.

Temperate deciduous forest   A major terrestrial environment on Earth with trees that shed their leaves in the fall and grow new leaves in the spring.

Terrarium   A container with plants growing inside.

Terrestrial   Refers to Earth's land environments.

Thrive   To grow and be healthy.

Tropical rain forest   A major terrestrial environment on Earth that is hot and wet all year.

Tundra   A major terrestrial environment on Earth where it is cold and dry.

Understory   The layer above the rain forest floor and below the rain forest canopy.

Vernal pool   A shallow, temporary pond.

Yeast   A type of fungus. Some types of yeast are used to make bread.

Zooplankton   Microscopic animals in aquatic environments. Insects and fish eat zooplankton.

Earth Sciences

Solid Earth

Earth Sciences
Table of Contents

Solid Earth

ES4b. Students know how to identify common rock-forming minerals (including quartz, calcite, feldspar, mica, and hornblende) and ore minerals by using a table of diagnostic properties.

What Geologists Do

D id you ever wonder what a **geologist** does? Geologists are scientists who study Earth. Geologists study **rocks** to learn their histories. They look for clues in rocks. When they study a rock, they try to figure out what it is made of and how it formed. They want to learn what has happened to the rock. Did the rock form from cooling **lava?** Did a stream or glacier move it?

Geologists working at a rock outcrop

Fieldwork

Geologists often begin their work outdoors. This is called fieldwork. They look for **outcrops** of rock to study. An outcrop is a place where Earth's **crust** is exposed. Earth's crust is the hard outer layer of solid rock. In most places the crust is hidden by soil, plants, water, and buildings. An outcrop is a good place to see what Earth is made of.

When a geologist finds an outcrop to study, she marks its position on a map. She makes observations and records them in her field notebook. She might take a picture or draw the outcrop. She makes notes about the color and texture of the rocks.

A geologist recording observations

Finally the geologist collects rock samples from the outcrop. That ends the fieldwork. The samples are taken to the geology lab. Lab work is the second part of what geologists do.

Lab Work

One of the most useful tools in the lab is a **microscope.** A microscope gives the geologist a close look at the rock sample's surface and its insides. To study the inside of a rock, the geologist must prepare the rock following these steps.

A diamond saw used to cut rocks

1. Slice off a thin piece of rock with a diamond saw. The piece is about a half centimeter (quarter inch) thick.

2. Use a grinding wheel covered with diamond dust to polish one side of the piece.

3. Glue the smooth side to a piece of glass to make a slide.

4. Use the diamond wheel again to grind down and polish the other side of the sample.

The sample is ready when it is so thin that light will shine through it. The slide is called a **thin section.**

The thin section is viewed with a microscope. The rock sample may have beautiful patterns of brightly colored shapes, like a stained glass window. The colors and shapes help the geologist figure out what the rock is made of and how it formed.

Geologists use other tools to find out how old rocks are. When the data have been collected, they use computers to organize and interpret the information.

A thin section viewed through a microscope

A geologist using a computer

Review Questions

1. **What are some of the ways geologists study rocks in the field?**

2. **What kind of information is important to include in a geologist's field notebook?**

3. **What are some of the tools that geologists use in the lab to study rocks?**

ES4b. Students know how to identify common rock-forming minerals (including quartz, calcite, feldspar, mica, and hornblende) and ore minerals by using a table of diagnostic properties.

Mock Rocks

A mock rock

Mock rocks. Are they rocks or are they something else?

The name says it all. The word *mock* has several meanings. *Mock* can mean making fun of something. If you imitate your friend and act in a silly way, you are mocking your friend. *Mock* can also mean fake. If you make "apple pie" using crackers instead of apples, you are making a mock apple pie. So *mock* can mean imitation or fake.

That's what a **mock rock** is. A mock rock is a fake rock or an imitation rock.

Rocks and Mock Rocks

A broken mock rock

Rocks are solid earth materials made of two or more ingredients. Rocks and mock rocks are both made out of several ingredients. The ingredients in rocks are **minerals.** The ingredients in mock rocks are sand, gravel, and flour. Sand, gravel, and flour are fake minerals.

A broken real rock

Rocks and mock rocks can be taken apart. Rocks are usually very hard. You need a hammer to break real rocks apart. Mock rocks are pretty soft. You can take them apart with your hands and a nail.

The pieces of minerals in rocks are sometimes so small that you need a powerful microscope to see them. The pieces of fake mineral in mock rocks are pretty large. Their **properties** of size, color, and shape make them easy to tell apart. You can see them with your bare eyes and a hand lens.

Some of the fake minerals in mock rocks **dissolve** when you add water. You can study the material that dissolves if you wait for the water to **evaporate.**

So why isn't a mock rock really a rock? Because real rocks are natural. They are found on hillsides, beaches, and deserts. They are found in rivers, lakes, and oceans. Mountains, cliffs, and volcanoes are made out of rock. Rocks can also be found in gardens, roads, and living rooms. If a rock is made by natural processes, it is a real rock.

Other Mock Rocks

You have probably seen other things that look like rocks. Bricks and concrete are hard as rock, and they are made from natural materials. But they are not rocks, because humans make them. The asphalt used to pave roads is hard, but humans make it. Even the colorful aquarium gravel in your mock rocks was made in a factory. It is not real rock either.

Brick and concrete

A pretend rock used to hide a key

Clever people also make other kinds of mock rocks. Have you seen soap, candles, and foam toys that look exactly like rocks? You can easily be fooled by these imitation rocks, until you hold one in your hand. Then it's clear. A rock is not a rock unless it is natural.

But the sand in mock rocks is a different story. Sand is tiny rocks. Each tiny particle of sand is a real rock. The sand particles were once part of a mountain or volcano.

Minerals

There are thousands of different kinds of rocks in the world. Some are shades of green and some are brown. Some rocks are gray with shiny pink and black dots, and some are streaked red and black.

Rocks with minerals you can see

Rocks look different because they are made of different minerals. A rock made of a black mineral and a white mineral will be black and white. If the rock has a lot of the white mineral, it might look white with black dots, streaks, or layers. If you hit a black-and-white rock with a hammer, the rock will break into tiny pieces of black mineral and white mineral.

At least 4,000 minerals have been identified on Earth. But most of these minerals are rare. About 25 minerals are common. They combine in different ways to form rocks. These 25 **rock-forming minerals** make most of the rocks found on Earth.

Minerals are pure earth materials. They are made of only one kind of material. If you break a mineral into bits with a hammer, each piece of mineral is the same as all the other pieces.

The different kinds and amounts of minerals in rocks make rocks different from one another.

A broken rock showing different minerals

A broken mineral showing uniformity

Review Questions

1. **What is the same about all rocks?**
2. **Why do rocks look different from one another?**

Crystal Identification Table

Crystals are the natural forms of many minerals. Crystals can help identify a mineral.

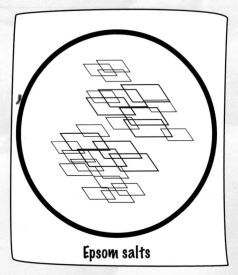

Epsom salts

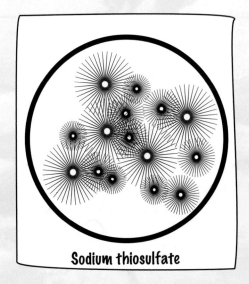

Sodium thiosulfate

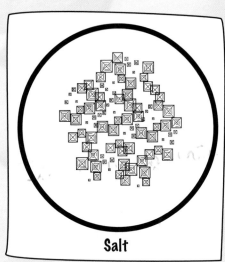

Salt

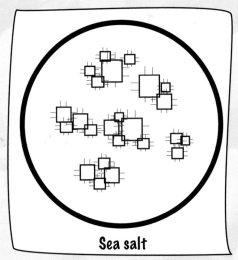

Sea salt

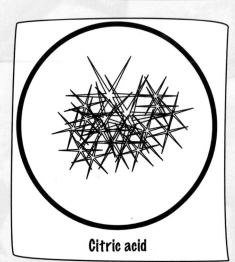

Citric acid

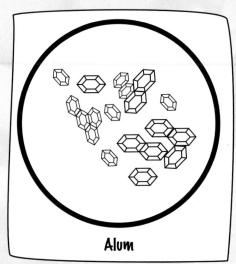

Alum

Summary: Mock Rocks

Geologists are scientists who study **rocks.** They begin their study of rocks outdoors. They look for rock **outcrops.** They observe rocks in the outcrop and write notes in their notebooks. Then they collect rock samples to study in the lab.

Rocks are usually made of two or more different kinds of materials. The materials, or ingredients, in rocks are called **minerals.** Geologists try to identify the **rock-forming minerals** in rocks. Then they come up with ideas about where the rocks came from.

Identifying minerals can be hard. Geologists observe many **properties** of minerals to tell them apart. One important property is the shape of a mineral's **crystal.**

Mock rocks are imitation rocks. They are easy to take apart and study. The mock rock ingredients are like the minerals in a real rock. Three of the fake minerals in mock rocks are gravel, sand, and flour.

The pieces of gravel and sand are large enough to see. Their properties of color, size, and shape make them easy to tell apart. Other ingredients in mock rocks are too small to see.

When you added water to the gray material, something in the mock rock **dissolved.** When the water **evaporated,** crystals appeared.

The Crystal Identification Table on page 186 shows the shape of crystals for six materials. The crystals in your evaporation dish had the same shape as the crystals in the "Salt" dish. The crystals were salt. Salt was an ingredient in your mock rock.

When you figured out what minerals were in your mock rock, you were doing the same work a geologist does.

Summary Questions

Now is a good time to review what you have recorded in your science notebook. Think about the investigations you have conducted with rocks and minerals.

1. **What do geologists do?**

2. **What are rocks made of?**

California Science Standard

ES4b. Students know how to identify common rock-forming minerals (including quartz, calcite, feldspar, mica, and hornblende) and ore minerals by using a table of diagnostic properties.

Vocabulary

geologist

rock

outcrop

mineral

rock-forming mineral

property

crystal

mock rock

dissolve

evaporate

Extensions

Math Problem of the Week

On his vacation, Jay hunted for rocks for his collection.

On the first day, he found two rocks. The next day he found four rocks.

On each day of his vacation, Jay found two more rocks than he had found the day before.

On what day did Jay have 42 rocks in his collection?

Jay's collection box can hold 5 kilograms of rocks. The average mass of a rock in Jay's collection is 200 grams. On what day will Jay have to get a second box to hold his rock collection?

Home/School Connection

Share a Rock Riddle

Make a rock collection. Choose from rocks you have at home. Or you can go outside and find some interesting rocks in your neighborhood. Try to get about ten rocks.

Put the rocks on a table. Give each person in your family a piece of paper and a pencil. Have everyone choose one rock to write about. But don't let anyone say which rock they have chosen. Have everyone write a riddle that describes one of the rocks.

Take turns reading the riddles out loud. Can everyone else figure out which rock the riddle is about? If they guess wrong, ask them what would help them guess correctly.

Bring your favorite rock riddle and the rock to school to share with the class. (Don't show it to anyone until your teacher tells you to!)

ES4b. Students know how to identify common rock-forming minerals (including quartz, calcite, feldspar, mica, and hornblende) and ore minerals by using a table of diagnostic properties.

Mining for Minerals

Gold

Do you know what a 49er is? That's the nickname given to people who poured into California in 1849. Why did they come? **Gold!**

Gold was discovered in a stream in Coloma, California, in 1848. It was in the form of nuggets. You could scoop up a pan full of stream gravel and wash the gravel away. This would leave the heavy gold in the pan. In a few years the California gold country was full of thousands of gold panners trying to strike it rich. Before too long the gold was panned out.

Was all the gold gone? No. The rocks still held a lot of gold **ore.** Ore is any rock or mineral that has a valuable substance in it. Gold ore has gold in it. Silver ore has silver. Iron ore has iron, and so on.

The search for gold changed from panning to mining. Gold miners used dynamite and shovels to get the ore. Sometimes they dug deep tunnels to get the gold. Big machines crushed the ore. The miners then separated the gold from the rest of the minerals.

Gold ore—gold and quartz

Bauxite

Bauxite is a rock. It is made of three minerals. Each of the minerals has the metal aluminum in it.

In many places around the world, bauxite is a red clay. Bauxite deposits found on or near Earth's surface are scooped up with big power shovels. The ore is crushed, screened, and ground into powder. Then heat and electricity separate aluminum out of the bauxite.

Aluminum is three times lighter than steel and almost as strong. It is a good material for building bridges, airplanes, bicycles, and cars. Because it does not rust, aluminum is made into boats and siding for houses. It is also made into wire, cans, kitchenware, and foil for wrapping food.

Aluminum ore—bauxite

Iron

The most important metal in the world is iron. Modern buildings, train tracks, ships, tools, cars, and thousands of other things are made of iron. Well, not iron exactly. Most iron is made into steel. Steel is the backbone of industry.

Iron is made from iron ore. The most common iron ore is a mineral called **hematite.** Huge furnaces heat the ore with charcoal and limestone. This is called **smelting.** The iron melts. The liquid iron is poured into molds. The raw iron is called pig iron.

A hematite mine

Iron ore—hematite

A furnace making pig iron

Pig iron is brittle, so it breaks easily. But by adding carbon to the iron, the iron becomes strong and flexible. Iron with carbon is steel.

Steel can be rolled into sheets. Sheet steel is used to make car bodies, refrigerators, and a lot of other things. Steel can be made into cutting tools with sharp edges. Steel can also be shaped into big beams to make large buildings. Nails and bolts that hold things together are made of steel.

Copper

Copper is the metal in pennies. It is also the most important metal used to make electric wires. Copper is one of the best conductors of electricity.

Copper ores are minerals. One of the best **ore minerals** is **malachite.** It is bright bluish green. Where copper ore is found near Earth's surface, it is broken apart with dynamite. The pieces are then loaded into trucks and taken to the smelter.

At the smelter the ore is put into a furnace. The heat melts the copper. It flows out the bottom of the furnace into molds. The copper is ready to make into wire, cooking pots, and pipes.

An open-pit copper mine

Copper ore—malachite

Loading copper ore

When copper is mixed with another metal called tin, it makes bronze. Bronze has been used for centuries to make things like church bells and statues. Why?

Bronze bells make a beautiful sound when they are struck. But there is another reason. Bells and statues are outdoors all the time. They get wet. Bronze does not rust like iron. Objects made of bronze are not changed by weather. A bronze statue will last for thousands of years.

Smelting copper ore

Review Questions

1. What is ore?

2. Which of the ores shown below could produce a metal you might find in a radio? Why do you think so?

3. Which ore could produce a metal that would make a good hammer? Why?

4. Which ore could produce a metal you would like to wear? Why?

5. Which ore could produce a metal that would make a good airplane wing? Why?

6. Identify the four ores shown below.

a.
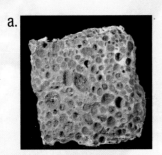

b.

c.

d.

ES4b. Students know how to identify common rock-forming minerals (including quartz, calcite, feldspar, mica, and hornblende) and ore minerals by using a table of diagnostic properties.

Birthstones

Geologists use a number scale to describe mineral **hardness.** Friedrich Mohs (1773–1839) came up with the scale. Mohs was a German scientist who studied minerals. He knew that some minerals could scratch others. If one mineral could scratch another, it must be harder than the mineral that was scratched.

The Mohs hardness scale goes from 1 (soft) to 10 (hard). The mineral talc, the softest mineral, has a hardness of 1. Diamond, the hardest mineral, has a hardness of 10. All the other minerals fall between talc and diamond. These ten minerals represent the ten levels of hardness.

Between the hardest and softest minerals are all the other minerals. Minerals with higher numbers on the Mohs scale will scratch minerals with lower numbers. **Calcite** can scratch gypsum, but it cannot scratch fluorite. **Quartz** can scratch **feldspar,** but it cannot scratch topaz.

Mohs hardness scale

10 Diamond
9 Corundum
8 Topaz
7 Quartz
6 Feldspar
5 Apatite
4 Fluorite
3 Calcite
2 Gypsum
1 Talc

The minerals at the hard end of the Mohs scale are called gems. **Gems** are hard minerals that can be cut into beautiful shapes. Because they are hard, they last a very long time.

People have identified gem minerals with the months of the year. These gems are called **birthstones.** At one time, people believed birthstones could protect, heal, or bring good luck. Some birthstones were thought to have magical powers. Which of these beautiful minerals is your birthstone?

January: Garnet
Often colored red, garnet crystals form easily in rock. Long ago, people believed a garnet would protect its owner from wounds.

February: Amethyst
Amethyst is a form of quartz that is purple. Amethysts were once thought to keep soldiers safe in battle.

March: Aquamarine
The mineral beryl forms crystals of different colors. Blue crystals are called aquamarines. Aquamarines were supposed to bring good luck to sailors at sea.

April: Diamond
It takes extreme heat and pressure to turn carbon into diamond. Diamond is the hardest natural substance in the world. Some people believed a diamond would give them strength.

May: Emerald
Unlike other gems, emeralds are not found washed into streams. They must be mined from other rock. It was said that an emerald placed under the tongue lets you see the future.

June: Alexandrite
Along with pearl, alexandrite is the birthstone for June. This mineral is both rare and unique. In natural sunlight it looks green. But when it is lit by a lightbulb, it looks red.

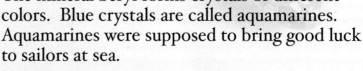

July: Ruby

Most rubies are found in streambeds or under soil. It was thought that a ruby turning dark warned its owner of danger.

August: Peridot

Green and yellow–green peridots are forms of the mineral olivine. They can be found in lava flows and in meteorites. Peridot is the only gem that may come from outer space! Peridot was said to give its wearer dignity.

September: Sapphire

Both sapphires (blue) and rubies (red) are crystals of the same mineral, corundum. Legend says a sapphire will make a foolish person wise.

October: Opal

Opals can be clear, cloudy, or **opaque.** Opals of good quality may show rainbowlike colors. The Romans wore opals for love and hope.

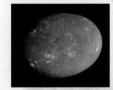

November: Topaz

Pure topaz is colorless. Impurities can make topaz yellow, blue, green, orange, or pink. In the Middle Ages, topaz was said to improve the mind. The largest known topaz crystal weighs 271 kilograms (596 pounds)!

December: Turquoise

Bluish green turquoise is an opaque mineral that is rarely found in crystal form. Native Americans of the Navajo tribe believed a turquoise thrown into a river with a prayer would bring rain.

Diamond is the hardest birthstone. How do you think the other birthstones measure up? Here is a list of birthstones from hardest to softest based on the Mohs scale.

- Diamond (10)
- Ruby and sapphire (9)
- Topaz (8)
- Alexandrite (8.5)
- Aquamarine and emerald (7.5-8)
- Garnet (7-7.5)
- Amethyst and peridot (6.5-7)
- Opal (5.5-6.5)
- Turquoise (5-6)

Review Questions

1. Where would an aluminum nail be on the Mohs scale? Why do you think so?

2. Where would a fingernail be on the Mohs scale? Why do you think so?

3. Steel will scratch apatite, but will not scratch feldspar. Where is steel on the Mohs scale?

4. Say you wanted to make a grinding wheel to sharpen steel tools. What mineral would you use to make it? Explain your answer.

Summary: Scratch Test

Minerals are earth materials. Minerals are pure substances. Minerals can be put into different groups. One is a group of minerals called gems. Your birthstone is one of the gem minerals.

Minerals are not usually found alone. They are usually mixed with other minerals to form rocks. **Quartz** and **feldspar** are two common rock-forming minerals.

Some minerals have ingredients that are valuable to people. Iron is an example of a valuable material in the mineral **hematite.** Minerals that people mine to get iron, aluminum, copper, and **gold** are called **ore minerals.**

Mineral Hardness

Identifying minerals can be difficult. Mineral **hardness** can help. Some minerals are hard, like quartz. Some minerals are soft, like gypsum. Geologists scratch minerals with steel and aluminum tools. If the tool makes a scratch, they know the tool is harder than the mineral.

Quartz	Fluorite	Calcite	Gypsum
Cannot be scratched with steel	Can be scratched with steel	Can be scratched with aluminum	Can be scratched with fingernail
Hardness = 7	Hardness = 4	Hardness = 3	Hardness = 2
A common mineral in Earth's crust	Appears in many colors	A common mineral in Earth's crust	Used to make plaster

Friedrich Mohs studied mineral hardness. He figured out a scale to help understand mineral hardness. He assigned 1 to talc, the softest mineral. He assigned 10 to diamond, the hardest mineral. All the other minerals are between talc and diamond.

A geologist's steel knife is 5.5 on the Mohs hardness scale. An aluminum nail is 3.5 on the Mohs scale. With these tools, geologists can find out a lot about the minerals they are trying to identify.

Summary Questions

Now is a good time to review what you have recorded in your science notebook. Think about the investigations you have conducted with rocks and minerals.

1. **Why is it important to observe more than one property of a mineral when you try to identify it?**

2. **If you found a new mineral, how would you find out its hardness?**

3. **What does it mean when we say calcite has a hardness of 3?**

California Science Standard

ES4b. Students know how to identify common rock-forming minerals (including quartz, calcite, feldspar, mica, and hornblende) and ore minerals by using a table of diagnostic properties.

Vocabulary

quartz

feldspar

hematite

gold

ore mineral

hardness

Extensions

Math Problem of the Week

Cheryl and Vincent were testing minerals for hardness. After working all day, they had tested 57 minerals. Cheryl tested nine more minerals than Vincent. How many minerals did each student test?

Vincent found that one-third of his minerals could be scratched with a paper clip, one-third with an aluminum nail, and one-third with his fingernail. Cheryl found the same results with the minerals she tested.

How many of the minerals were scratched with each tool?

Home/School Connection

Birthstones

Tell your family what you learned about birthstones and the difference between rocks and minerals.

Ask family and friends when their birthday is. See if they know their birthstone. (If they don't, you can tell them!) Make a chart like the one below. Then make a bar graph to show which month has the most birthdays.

Name of person	Birthday month
_____	_____
_____	_____
_____	_____
_____	_____
_____	_____
_____	_____

Garnet	Amethyst	Aquamarine	Diamond	Emerald	Alexandrite	Ruby	Peridot	Sapphire	Opal	Topaz	Turquoise

ES4b. Students know how to identify common rock-forming minerals (including quartz, calcite, feldspar, mica, and hornblende) and ore minerals by using a table of diagnostic properties.

Calcite = Calcium Carbonate

Calcite is a mineral found in many of Earth's rocks. Calcite is also called calcium carbonate. It is in a group of minerals called **carbonates.** The carbonates are one of the largest groups of minerals. All carbonates contain carbon and oxygen.

A rock being tested for calcite

How can you find out if a rock contains calcite? Put a few drops of **acid** on it. If the rock bubbles and fizzes, then the rock contains calcite. Calcite fizzes when acid touches it. It is the only common mineral that fizzes.

Geologists take a small bottle of acid with them in the field. When they put a drop of acid on a rock that contains calcite, it fizzes quickly. That's **evidence** that the rock contains calcite.

Testing rocks for calcite

Vinegar is a common acid around the home. When you put calcite in vinegar, you get a **chemical reaction.** The acid breaks down the calcite. This reaction creates carbon dioxide gas. That's what is inside the bubbles. The bubbles are not air bubbles, they are carbon dioxide bubbles. Do you know where else carbon dioxide bubbles are common? In soda drinks.

Calcite Properties

Calcite has some other interesting properties. Some forms of calcite are **transparent.** One form is called Iceland spar. When you place a piece of Iceland spar on a printed word, you see a double image. Can you see two images in the photo below?

Iceland spar   Dog-tooth calcite

Another form of calcite has pointed crystals. It is called dog-tooth calcite. Can you see where it gets this name?

Calcite Everywhere

Calcite is a common rock-forming mineral on Earth. But you may not know it when you see it. Here are some places you might see this mineral.

Did you know that **chalk** is a form of calcite? Chalk is made of tiny pieces of calcite that formed in shallow seas. In some places, chalk forms tall cliffs, as in the photo to the right.

Limestone is made mostly of calcite. Limestone is a **sedimentary rock.** That means limestone forms in layers when calcium carbonate settles on the bottom of oceans and bays.

Marble is also made of calcite because it is made from limestone. Marble is a **metamorphic rock.** That means marble is formed by heat and pressure. Limestone changes into marble when pressure and heat act on it for a long time. Marble is a common building rock. The Washington Monument in Washington, DC, is made of marble.

Have you ever been in a cave? If so, you might have seen rock formations called **stalactites.** Stalactites hang from the cave ceiling and contain calcite. Sometimes stalactites form tufa columns from the ceiling to the floor. The rock is called **tufa.**

Washington Monument

Stalactites made of tufa in a cave

Another sedimentary rock that contains calcite is **travertine.** You can find travertine around hot springs, like the ones at Yellowstone National Park. Polished travertine can be used for jewelry and sculptures.

A polished travertine sculpture

Travertine around a hot spring

Review Questions

1. **Why do geologists carry a small bottle of weak acid in the field?**

2. **Why does calcite fizz?**

3. **What kinds of rock contain calcite?**

4. **What do you think happens when acid rain (rain containing weak acid) falls on a marble monument like the Washington Monument?**

ES4a. Students know how to differentiate among igneous, sedimentary, and metamorphic rocks by referring to their properties and methods of formation (the rock cycle).

Rock of Ages

Humans build monuments to remember important people and events. Monuments are built to last a long time. They are usually large structures. If you were going to build a monument, what would you make it out of? Rock would be a good choice.

From ancient times to the present, people have made monuments out of rock. Why? Because rock is found everywhere. Rock can be cut and shaped. And most of all, rock lasts a long time. Some rocks are nearly as old as Earth itself. Some structures made of rock have been standing for thousands of years.

The Great Pyramid of Egypt

206

The Great Pyramid

Did you know that the Great Pyramid in Egypt is almost completely solid? The only spaces inside are a few hallways and rooms. The pyramid is made out of about 2,300,000 blocks of limestone and **granite!** The average block weighs about as much as two cars. The largest blocks weigh as much as six cars.

As big as it is, the Great Pyramid was made to honor just one person. It was built around 2700 B.C.E. to hold the body of the pharaoh Khufu. He was a ruler of ancient Egypt.

Each building block in the pyramid was pulled to the site on a wooden sled. Workers used copper axes, chisels, and saws to cut and fit the stones. Today people wonder how such a building was made without iron tools.

Limestone for the pyramid's center was cut from nearby cliffs. That way, the stone did not have to be moved very far. Granite for the walls and doorways came from almost 1,000 kilometers (600 miles) up the Nile River. Better limestone for the outside of the pyramid was floated down the river from a few kilometers away. Today the original limestone shell is gone. The stone was "recycled" in the 1300s to rebuild a city damaged by earthquakes.

What Is Limestone?

Limestone is a sedimentary rock that forms from calcium carbonate. Limestone forms under water. Tiny bits of calcium carbonate drift to the bottom of oceans or bays. These pieces of calcium carbonate pile up for millions of years. The layer of calcium carbonate gets thicker and thicker. After a very long time, the bits of calcium carbonate turn into limestone.

Look at the picture of the Great Pyramid on page 206. Where is the water? Long gone. Limestone is found on Earth's surface millions of years after it forms under water.

The Taj Mahal

What Is Marble?

Marble is a metamorphic rock. Metamorphic rocks form when one kind of rock changes into another kind of rock. This usually happens when heat and pressure act on a rock for a long time.

Marble starts out as limestone. When limestone gets buried deep in the earth, the pressure builds. The temperature goes up. After millions of years, the limestone changes into marble.

The Taj Mahal

The Taj Mahal in Agra, India, is one of the eight wonders of the world. Many agree that it is the most beautiful building of all time. The Taj Mahal's designer was Emperor Shah Jahan. He built the monument to honor his wife, Mumtaz Mahal, who died in 1631.

The Taj Mahal, which means "Crown Palace," is made entirely of white marble. Builders from all over the Middle East worked 22 years to make it. Inside the Taj Mahal, colorful marble was cut and pieced together like a puzzle. Forty-three different kinds of gemstones were used for decoration.

The Vietnam Veterans Memorial

The Taj Mahal and the Great Pyramid each honor a single person. The Vietnam Veterans Memorial was built to remember all the Americans who died in the Vietnam War (1955–1975). It was the idea of Vietnam veteran Jan Scruggs.

A competition was held to design the memorial. Maya Ying Lin's plan was chosen. At the time, Lin was 21 years old. She was a student at Yale University. Lin designed the monument as a black granite wall. The wall forms a V. She wanted the rock to rise out of the ground like two arms to embrace people. One arm points to the Washington Monument. The other arm points to the Lincoln Memorial.

The wall was finished in 1982. The names of more than 58,000 military men and women are written on the wall. Many people didn't like Lin's design at the time. But the memorial she designed is one of the most visited sites in Washington, DC.

What Is Granite?

Granite is an **igneous rock**. That means it started as melted rock deep under Earth's surface. As the melted rock moved toward the surface, it cooled and crystallized. When you look closely at granite, you can see the crystals of the different minerals.

There are only a few places in the world where black granite is found. The beautiful black granite in the Vietnam Veterans Memorial comes from India.

Designer Maya Ying Lin and visitors at the Vietnam Veterans Memorial

The California Capitol

The California State Capitol

In 1860, construction began on the new state capitol in Sacramento, California. The design called for both iron and rock. Iron would be used to build the frame. Granite would cover the outside. The outer shell of granite would make the capitol building strong and beautiful.

That was the plan. But that's not what happened. The first winter it poured rain and the foundations flooded. The construction was off to a bad start.

Over the next few years there was progress. In 1865, the first level was completed. And the granite outer surface was attached. Things looked pretty good.

But soon there was more trouble. The cost of the building was going up. To save money, plaster was put on the outside walls.

Finally, in 1874, construction was complete. The iron columns and upper-level surfaces were made to look like granite. The grand stairs leading up to the entrance and the interior staircase were granite. The floors were polished marble. And more than 125 years later, the building still looks great.

The California State Capitol combines modern building methods and age-old building materials.

Review Questions

1. **Why do people use rock to build monuments?**

2. **Which of the monuments in this article used sedimentary rock? Metamorphic rock? Igneous rock?**

3. **How do sedimentary, metamorphic, and igneous rocks form?**

Summary: Calcite Quest

Calcite is a mineral made from calcium carbonate. It has an interesting property. Calcite fizzes or bubbles when placed in a weak acid, like vinegar. No other common mineral does this.

When calcite is placed in vinegar, it dissolves and bubbles. The bubbles are carbon-dioxide gas. When the vinegar evaporates, a white residue is left in the dish.

Calcite is a common mineral in rocks. You can find out if a rock has calcite by putting it in acid. If it fizzes, the rock contains calcite. The **limestone** and **marble** you investigated are examples of rocks that contain calcite. **Chalk** in cliffs, **tufa** in caves, and **travertine** in hot springs also contain calcite. Basalt and granite are rocks that don't contain calcite.

Calcite is common in **sedimentary** and **metamorphic rocks.** Sedimentary rocks form when bits of rock and mineral settle to the bottom of oceans and bays. After a long time, the layers of sediments turn into rock. When calcium carbonate is one of the sediments, the rock will contain calcite.

Limestone is a sedimentary rock made mostly of calcite. When heat and pressure change limestone, it becomes the metamorphic rock marble.

Calcite is rare in **igneous rocks.** Igneous rocks, such as **granite,** form from melted minerals deep under Earth's surface. When the melted minerals move toward Earth's surface, they cool and crystallize.

Rock has been used to build monuments for thousands of years. The Great Pyramid in Egypt is a structure that has stood for 4,700 years. Do you think the California State Capitol will stand for 4,700 years?

Summary Questions

Now is a good time to review what you have recorded in your science notebook. Think about the investigations you have conducted with rocks and minerals.

1. **Which property of calcite makes it easy to identify?**

2. **What are some of the rocks that contain calcite?**

3. **What are the three types of rocks? How does each type form?**

Vocabulary

limestone

marble

chalk

tufa

travertine

sedimentary rock

metamorphic rock

igneous rock

granite

Extensions

Math Problem of the Week

Josh and Paris were playing the game rock, scissors, and paper. (Rock crushes scissors, scissors cuts paper, paper covers rock.) They had agreed that at the end of each game, the loser would give the winner a rock from his or her collection.

After playing many games, Josh had won three games and Paris had won the rest. When they stopped playing, Paris had three more rocks than she had when they began.

What is the fewest games of rock, scissors, and paper they could have played?

Home/School Connection

Calcite Test

Explain to members of your family how geologists test rocks to see if they contain the mineral calcite. Take a short walk with your family. See if you can find five or six rocks to test for calcite.

Carefully test the rocks with vinegar. Record your findings.

Do not test special rocks, such as fancy crystals or valuable rocks. The vinegar could change their appearance and lessen their value.

ES4b. Students know how to identify common rock-forming minerals (including quartz, calcite, feldspar, mica, and hornblende) and ore minerals by using a table of diagnostic properties.

Identifying Minerals

Rocks are made out of earth materials called minerals. Minerals can be colorful and beautiful.

Minerals come in many colors. Look at the photo below. Start with the brown mineral at the top and move clockwise. The minerals shown are copper, orpiment/realgar, beryl, malachite, sapphire, olivine, and cinnabar. The yellow mineral in the center is sulfur.

Samples of eight colorful minerals

Many kinds of rock can be made out of just a few kinds of minerals. Geologists try to find out what kinds of minerals are in rocks. They use property tables to help them identify the minerals they find in rocks. Here are some of the mineral properties they use.

Hardness

Hardness is determined by trying to scratch a mineral with different materials. Minerals with large hardness numbers, like 8 and 9, can't be scratched except with a diamond. Even a steel knife won't scratch a hard mineral. Minerals with small hardness numbers, like 1 and 2, are easy to scratch. A fingernail can scratch one of these minerals.

A scientist might use a nail to test the hardness of a mineral like this feldspar.

Color

Some minerals, such as black biotite mica, have colors that help identify them. But many minerals come in several colors. The property of color does not always help identify a mineral.

Fluorite is a mineral that comes in many colors.

Luster

Luster describes the way light reflects off a mineral's surface. The simple way to describe a mineral's luster is **metallic** or **nonmetallic.** Metallic luster means the mineral shines like a metal. Nonmetallic means it does not shine like metal. The mineral could be glassy, pearly, or dull. The pyrite shown below has a metallic luster. The calcite and fluorite have nonmetallic lusters.

Iron pyrite has metallic luster.
Calcite and fluorite have nonmetallic lusters.

Magnetism

A mineral is **magnetic** if it is attracted to a magnet. Lodestone is a special form of the mineral magnetite that acts as a magnet itself. Lodestone was used in some of the first compasses because of its magnetic property.

Steel nails stick to this magnetic mineral.

Cleavage

Regular, flat surfaces on broken minerals are called **cleavage.** Some minerals only **fracture.** That means when they break, the surfaces are uneven, rounded, or splintered. Calcite shows cleavage. Quartz and the rock obsidian show rounded and uneven fractures.

Cleavage surfaces are smooth and flat in this mineral.

Rounded fractures on obsidian

Uneven fractures on quartz

Streak

If you rub a mineral on a tile, it can leave some mineral powder. This is called **streak.** The color of the streak can help a geologist identify the mineral. Streak is usually a better property to use than the color of the mineral sample. Color varies within some minerals. But streak color is usually the same for all samples of one kind of mineral.

The mineral hematite leaves a reddish brown streak.

Mineral Properties Table

Mineral	Color	Hardness	Streak	Luster	Cleavage	Other properties
Calcite	colorless, white, gray	3	white	nonmetallic	yes	Fizzes in acid Double refraction
Feldspar	white, pink, gray	6	white	nonmetallic	yes	
Fluorite	clear, purple, yellow, colorless, green	4	white	nonmetallic	yes	Glows under a black light
Galena	dark gray	2.5	gray	metallic	yes	Heavy for its size
Gold	yellow	2.5 to 3	golden yellow	metallic	no	Very heavy for its size
Graphite	dark gray to black	1 to 2	black	metallic	yes	Feels greasy
Gypsum	colorless, white, gray	2	white	nonmetallic	yes	Can form rosettes or fibers
Hematite	brown, red, black	5 to 6	reddish brown	metallic or nonmetallic	no	Can appear glittery with a bright metallic luster, or dark brown or red with a dull luster
Hornblende	dark green, brown, black	5 to 6	white or gray	nonmetallic	yes	Crystals may be long with parallel sides
Magnetite	black	5.5 to 6.5	black	metallic	no	Attracted to a magnet
Malachite	dark green, light green	3.5 to 4	pale green	nonmetallic	no	Silky luster Bubbles with strong acid
Mica	dark brown, black, white	2 to 3	colorless	nonmetallic	yes	Pulls apart in sheets
Pyrite	yellow	6 to 6.5	greenish black	metallic	no	Also known as fool's gold
Quartz	colorless, white, rose, gray, purple, brown	7	colorless	nonmetallic	no	
Talc	white, greenish to gray	1	white	nonmetallic	yes	Feels greasy May pull apart in fibers

218

Review Questions

Use the Mineral Properties Table on page 218 to answer these questions.

1. How can you tell the difference between gold and pyrite?

2. How can you tell the difference between calcite and quartz?

3. How can you tell the difference between talc and gypsum?

4. A mineral sample is dark gray, can be scratched with a fingernail, has a metallic luster, and feels greasy. Which mineral is it?

INVESTIGATION 4

ES4a. Students know how to differentiate among igneous, sedimentary, and metamorphic rocks by referring to their properties and methods of formation (the rock cycle).

Where Do Rocks Come From?

Where do rocks come from? This question keeps geologists busy. Even though they don't have all the answers, they know a lot about where rocks come from.

There are three big groups of rocks. All the rocks in a group have similar origins. The three groups are igneous, sedimentary, and metamorphic.

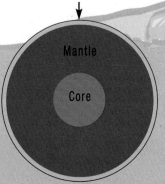

Cross section of Earth

Earth is like an egg. An egg has a hard outer layer called shell. Earth has a hard outer layer called crust. Earth's crust is made of solid rock.

Under the egg's shell is the fluid egg white. Under Earth's solid crust is the **mantle,** which flows like toothpaste. It's hot inside Earth. It is so hot that rocks and minerals melt.

The egg has a yolk in the center. Earth has a metal **core** in its center.

Igneous Rocks

Igneous rocks start out as melted rock in Earth's mantle. Sometimes the melted rock, called **magma,** comes to the surface in **volcanoes.** It pours out as lava. When the lava cools and hardens, it forms new rocks. The basalt you tested for calcite is volcanic igneous rock. The Cascade Mountains in northern California are mostly basalt rocks.

Other times, melted rock cools slowly and hardens below the surface. **Earthquakes** and other changes in Earth's crust might bring these igneous rocks to the surface years later. The granite you studied cooled below Earth's surface. The Sierra Nevada in central California are mostly granite mountains.

Sedimentary Rocks

Sedimentary rocks form from bits and pieces of recycled rocks and minerals. **Sandstone** is an example of a sedimentary rock. Sandstone starts as big rocks in mountains. Over time, the rocks crack and break into smaller pieces. This process is called **weathering.**

Water can cause weathering in rocks. Water freezes in cracks in rocks. Water expands when it freezes, breaking the rocks apart. Tree roots also cause weathering. Roots reach into cracks in rocks. As the roots grow, big pieces of rock break loose.

Tree roots breaking rock

Loose rocks tumble downhill and break into smaller pieces. Pieces might end up in streams and rivers. The pieces get banged around and broken into smaller and smaller pieces. Eventually the rocks from the mountain are reduced to sand.

Sand often ends up in oceans and bays. Layers of sand build up. The layers of sand are called **sediment.** As millions of years pass, the sand gets buried under more layers of sediment. Sand particles are pressed and cemented together. The sand turns into the sedimentary rock sandstone.

Sandstone

Sedimentary rocks often have bits of sand and gravel you can see. Sometimes sedimentary rocks contain **fossils** of shells or plants. Sedimentary rocks form in layers. If the rocks are still in their natural site, you can often see the layers.

Metamorphic Rocks

Meta- means change. *Morph* means shape or form. Metamorphic rocks change from one kind of rock into another kind of rock. The starting rocks can be igneous, sedimentary, or even other metamorphic rocks. The rocks change because of heat and pressure. If a rock gets buried deep in Earth's crust or touches hot lava, it will change into metamorphic rock.

Heat and pressure can turn sandstone into quartzite. Limestone can become marble. Shale can change into slate. Heat and pressure can turn granite into gneiss (pronounced nice).

The Rock Cycle

Over time, one kind of rock can change into any other kind of rock. The changes from igneous to sedimentary to metamorphic and back to igneous are the **rock cycle.**

For example, a piece of igneous granite might weather into sediments. The sediments can end up in a layer with other sediments. After a long time, the sediments might change into sedimentary sandstone.

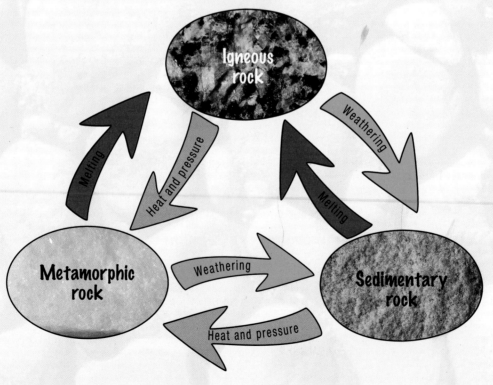

Any kind of rock can change into any other kind of rock. This is the rock cycle.

The sandstone could get heated by a lava flow or buried under other sediments. The heat and pressure might change the sandstone into metamorphic quartzite. And finally, the quartzite might be carried down into Earth's mantle where it will melt. After millions of years, the rock material might come back as a new piece of igneous granite.

Rocks don't all follow this path through the rock cycle. The important thing to remember is that all rocks change. Any rock can change into any other kind of rock. Study the rock cycle illustration on page 222 to see how.

It is even possible for a rock to re-form as the same kind of rock. For example, sandstone might weather into sand. The sand could pile up in a bay. After millions of years, the sand might become new sandstone.

Or metamorphic rocks could get buried deep underground. The heat and pressure could change the metamorphic rocks into new metamorphic rocks.

Can you figure out how igneous rocks could change into new igneous rocks?

The chart on the next page shows several examples of sedimentary, igneous, and metamorphic rocks. How many of them have you held in your hand? Think about the changes these rocks might have gone through long before they came into your classroom.

Review Questions

1. **How do igneous rocks form?**

2. **How do sedimentary rocks form?**

3. **How do metamorphic rocks form?**

4. **Explain how a metamorphic rock could change into a sedimentary rock.**

5. **What kind of rocks often contain fossils?**

Rock Samples

Sedimentary	Igneous	Metamorphic
Limestone	Basalt	Marble
Sandstone	Granite	Quartzite
Shale	Tuff	Slate
Conglomerate	Pumice	Gneiss
Breccia	Obsidian	Schist

Summary: Take It for Granite

Streak, hardness, luster, and **cleavage.** What are we talking about?

Mineral properties. When a geologist finds a new mineral, she tests it. She observes the streak it leaves on a tile. She tests the hardness with tools. She looks to see how light reflects off its surface. She breaks the mineral and observes the pieces.

The geologist then compares her notes with a table of mineral properties. She looks for a description in the table that matches her observations. When she finds a match, she knows what kind of mineral she has found.

Rocks are made from minerals. Identifying minerals is one step in identifying rocks. But sometimes identifying minerals doesn't answer all the questions. Sometimes it raises more questions.

Sandstone and quartzite are two different kinds of rock. But sandstone and quartzite are both made of quartz. How can two rocks made of the same minerals be different?

Rocks that contain quartz **weather** into grains of sand called **sediments.** The quartz sand form layers in oceans and bays. After millions of years, the sediments stick together to form sandstone. Sandstone is a sedimentary rock.

Sometimes sandstone gets pushed deep into Earth's **crust.** The pressure and temperature build. Heat and pressure change the sandstone into the metamorphic rock quartzite. Quartzite is made of the same minerals as sandstone, but it is a different kind of rock.

225

When quartzite gets pushed down through the crust, it enters the **mantle.** The quartzite may melt and become part of the **magma.** Sometime in the future the minerals in the sandstone might come to the surface in a lava flow. When the lava cools, it will form new igneous rock.

The changes from one kind of rock to another is called the **rock cycle.**

Summary Questions

Now is a good time to review what you have recorded in your science notebook. Think about the investigations you have conducted with rocks and minerals.

1. **Which of these minerals doesn't go with the others? Quartz, feldspar, fluorite, hornblende. Why do you think so?**

2. **Which of these rocks doesn't go with the others? Pumice, sandstone, obsidian, granite. Why do you think so?**

3. **Describe the rock cycle.**

California Science Standards

ES4a. Students know how to differentiate among igneous, sedimentary, and metamorphic rocks by referring to their properties and methods of formation (the rock cycle).

ES4b. Students know how to identify common rock-forming minerals (including quartz, calcite, feldspar, mica, and hornblende) and ore minerals by using a table of diagnostic properties.

Vocabulary

streak

hardness

luster

cleavage

weathering

sediment

crust

mantle

magma

rock cycle

Extensions

Math Problem of the Week

Anders, Betty, Catherine, Dustin, Erik, and Felicia are rock collectors. Each collector has chosen some rocks from his or her collection to trade. Each collector is going to trade with every other collector.

How many different pairs of collectors will trade rocks?

Home/School Connection

Earth Materials Hunt

Use the clues to find items around your home that are made of earth materials.

- See if you can find something made from bauxite. Bauxite (aluminum) can be refined into a very thin metal good for packaging liquids.

- See if you can find something beautiful that someone might wear that is made from an earth material.

- Sometimes people use earth materials to make lamps and other decorative items for the home. Can you find something like that?

- Look at the thermometer you use to find out if you have a fever when you're sick. Which part of the thermometer do you think is made from earth materials?

- Look outside. Can you find something that you walk on every day that is made from earth materials?

- Can you think of a place that you have visited that had some interesting rocks or minerals? What is the name of the place? What was so interesting?

- There is an earth material that most people eat all the time. Imagine that! Its mineral name is halite. It's shaped like little white cubes, and you use it a lot in cooking.

INVESTIGATION 5

ES5b. Students know natural processes, including freezing and thawing and the growth of roots, cause rocks to break down into smaller pieces.

Weathering

Pebbles and sand are pieces of rock. Pebbles are pretty big, but pieces of sand are tiny. All rocks start out as huge masses of rock the size of mountains. How do mountains break down into pebbles and sand?

The answer is weathering. Weathering is the breaking apart of rocks into smaller pieces. Weathering happens to all rocks when they are **exposed** to water and air.

Physical weathering of cliffs

Physical Weathering

Rocks break down in two ways. **Physical weathering** makes rocks smaller, but does not change the rocks in any other way. When a big rock falls from the side of a cliff, it breaks into lots of little rocks. All the minerals in the little rocks are the same as the minerals in the big rock.

Rocks weathered by freezing and thawing of water

When rocks get hot and then cold, they can crack. Sometimes water gets into cracks in rocks. Water expands when it freezes. It can expand enough to break the rock along the crack. When the ice thaws and melts, the rock may fall into smaller pieces.

Tree roots grow and break rocks.

Roots of trees and bushes can reach down into cracks in rocks. As the roots grow, they make the cracks bigger. Sometimes the cracks get so big, the rock falls apart.

When rocks bang into one another, they get worn down. Rubbing, grinding, and banging is called **abrasion,** a kind of physical weathering. Abrasion happens when rocks fall in **landslides,** tumble in flowing water, or crash around in **waves.** Wind can blow sand against rocks. This sandblasting weathers the rocks.

Sand abrasion on cliffs

Blowing sand can weather rocks into interesting shapes.

Chemical weathering happens when minerals in rocks are changed by chemicals in water and air. The starting minerals change into new minerals.

Most rocks contain iron. When oxygen in the air comes in contact with iron, the iron in the rock can rust. Rust is iron oxide. Iron oxide is softer than other iron minerals. This causes the rock to break apart faster.

Chemical weathering of a rock containing iron

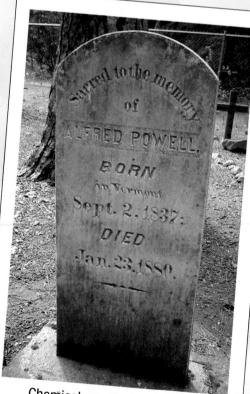

Chemical weathering of marble by acid rain

Carbon dioxide gas in the air dissolves in water droplets. This makes acid. The acid droplets can fall as rain. The acid causes the calcite in limestone and marble rocks to change chemically, and holes form. Monuments, buildings, and gravestones made of marble or limestone change and weaken when exposed to acid rain.

Salt can cause chemical weathering. Salt water can **react** with minerals in rocks to make new minerals. When the new minerals are softer than the original mineral, holes can form. The weak rock breaks and falls apart more easily.

Chemical weathering of sandstone by seawater

Review Questions

1. **What is the difference between physical and chemical weathering?**

2. **How do living organisms contribute to the weathering of rocks?**

3. **How does acid rain cause weathering?**

4. **How does ice cause weathering?**

Landform Vocabulary

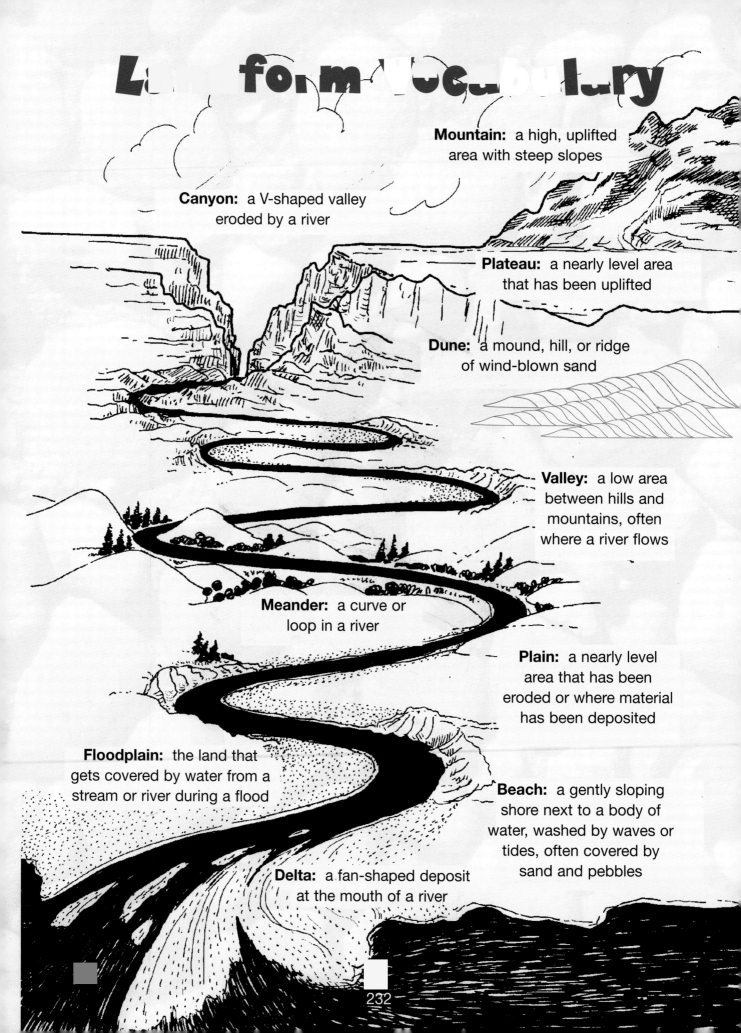

Mountain: a high, uplifted area with steep slopes

Canyon: a V-shaped valley eroded by a river

Plateau: a nearly level area that has been uplifted

Dune: a mound, hill, or ridge of wind-blown sand

Valley: a low area between hills and mountains, often where a river flows

Meander: a curve or loop in a river

Plain: a nearly level area that has been eroded or where material has been deposited

Floodplain: the land that gets covered by water from a stream or river during a flood

Beach: a gently sloping shore next to a body of water, washed by waves or tides, often covered by sand and pebbles

Delta: a fan-shaped deposit at the mouth of a river

ES5c. Students know moving water erodes landforms, reshaping the land by taking it away from some places and depositing it as pebbles, sand, silt, and mud in other places (weathering, transport, and deposition).

Erosion and Deposition

A trip to the beach is fun. One of the best parts is playing in the sand. And there is so much sand. Where did it all come from? Was it made right there or did it come from some other place?

A quartz sand beach in Carmel, California

Most of the sand on the beach came from the mountains. **Erosion** moved the sand from the mountains to the beach. Erosion is the taking away of weathered rock. After rocks have weathered into small pieces, gravity, water, wind, or ice can carry them away. Most of the sand on the beach in the photo was carried there by water flowing in rivers and streams.

As long as water keeps flowing, the bits of sand keep moving downstream. When the river enters the ocean, the water stops flowing. The sand settles to the bottom of the ocean. The settling of sediments is called **deposition.** Deposits of sand form beaches all over the world.

Erosion

The beach sand starts on high cliffs like those shown in the photo. Sometimes big chunks of rock fall off mountain cliffs. Gravity pulls rocks downhill. Other times landslides move rocks and soil downhill. The piles of rock at the bottom of cliffs are called talus or scree.

Cliffs high in the mountains

Weathered rock in a mountain creek

Rainwater moving over the ground erodes the broken rock. Water **transports** rock into creeks. Water flowing in creeks transports broken rock downstream. This is erosion.

Creeks flow into rivers. Rivers have strong currents. Rivers can carry many sizes of rock. The rocks bang together and rub on the riverbed. The rocks break into smaller and smaller pieces. These pieces are pebbles, gravel, sand, and silt.

Strong river current moves rocks downstream.

Pebbles at the edge of a river

The erosion continues. The farther the rocks move in the river, the smaller they get. They also get smoother and rounder as they tumble along.

Deposition

When the water flowing in a river slows down, it deposits sediments. Large rocks are the first to settle to the bottom. After a flood, large boulders can be scattered all around.

Large and small sediments deposited after a flood

Can you see deposits of sand and silt where this river enters the lake?

Where a river flows into a lake, bay, or ocean, the water stops moving. Sand is deposited near the mouth of the river. The sand can form sandbars, deltas, and beaches. Farther out are deposits of silt and clay.

San Francisco Bay Delta. Can you see meanders in the river where it crosses the delta?

Wind blows sand and small pieces of rock from one place to another. Sometimes the wind blows hard enough to carry a lot of sand and dust. Wind can erode valuable farmland.

A large dust storm approaching Spearman, Texas, in 1935

When the wind dies down, sand and dust are deposited far from their starting places. This is how sand dunes form. Death Valley and Imperial Valley are two places in California where large sand dunes form.

Sand dunes in
Death Valley National Monument

Imperial Dunes in California near the
Mexican border

Glaciers are frozen rivers. Rocks can be frozen in glaciers high in mountain canyons. Glaciers flow slowly down canyons. The frozen rocks scrape the floor and sides of the canyon. Glaciers erode V-shaped valleys into U-shaped valleys.

A U-shaped valley eroded by glaciers in the Sierra Nevada in California

Thousands of years ago in California, glaciers scraped down mountain valleys. They crushed and ground up rock beneath them. This physical weathering helped create the rich soil in the Central Valley between the cities of Bakersfield and Redding.

What happens when sand finally makes it to the ocean? Is that the end of the erosion and deposition story? Not quite. Waves erode beaches and deposit sand in different places all the time. As waves crash on the beach, sand continues to weather. Sand gets finer and finer. Sand abrades the rocks and cliffs along the ocean shore. Erosion and deposition go on and on.

Sand deposited on a northern California beach around a weathered rock

Review Questions

1. **Describe three ways rock is eroded and three ways rock is deposited.**

2. **Describe how rocks in the Cascade Mountains become sand on a beach along the California coast.**

3. **What do you think will happen to the Sierra Nevada in California in the next hundred million years?**

4. **What is the role of erosion and deposition in the rock cycle?**

Landforms Photo Album

Landforms Formed by Weathering and Erosion

Exfoliation dome: a dome formed when rocks like granite peel away at Earth's surface.

Spheroidal rocks: rounded rocks formed by physical and chemical weathering.

Arch: a curved rock that forms when chemical and/or physical weathering weakens the center, and the rock erodes.

Canyon: a V-shaped gorge with steep sides eroded by a stream.

Arches can form on land, as in Arches National Park, or near the coast where waves batter and erode the centers.

Gorge: a narrow, steep-sided valley or canyon.

Butte: a hill with steep sides and a small flat top. A butte is smaller than a mesa.

Hanging valley: a valley floor above another valley floor. Glacial erosion causes hanging valleys.

240

Hoodoo: weak rocks erode away, leaving behind the stronger rocks. Hoodoos can look like mushrooms or statues.

Mesa: a single, wide, flat-topped hill having at least one steep side.

Meander: a curve or loop in a river or stream.

Valley: a low area between mountains where a stream or glacier flows. Stream valleys are V-shaped. Glacier valleys are often U-shaped.

Landforms Formed by Deposition

Alluvial fan: a fan-shaped deposit of rocks formed where a stream flows from a steep slope onto flatter land.

Floodplain: land covered by water during a flood. Small particles, like sand and silt, are deposited on a floodplain.

Beach: an area made of sand and other sizes of rock between the low-tide level and the high-tide level.

Landslide: the rapid downslope movement of earth material.

Delta: a fan-shaped deposit of earth materials at the mouth of a stream.

Levee: a bank along a stream that may stop land from flooding. Levees can be natural or made by people.

Moraine: the unsorted rocks and soil carried and deposited by a glacier.

Sand dune: the sand deposited by wind in ridges, mounds, or hills.

Outwash plain: a flat or gently sloping surface made of sorted sediments deposited by water from melting glaciers.

Sandbar: a long ridge of sand in shallow water built up by river currents or ocean waves.

Plain: a low area of Earth's surface that is often formed of flat-lying sediments.

Slump: a downward movement of a single mass of earth material.

Landforms Formed by Eruptions

Volcano: a place where lava, cinders, ash, and gases pour out through openings in Earth's surface.

Cinder cone: a volcano formed from a pile of cinders and other volcanic material blown out in an explosive eruption.

Caldera: a hole that forms when the top of a volcano blows off or when the magma below the volcano drains away.

Composite volcano: a volcano built by alternating eruptions of lava, cinders, and ash. Mt. Shasta and Mt. Lassen in California are composite volcanoes.

Shield volcano: a volcano built of very fluid lava. It looks wider than it is tall. Shield volcanoes are found in the Hawaiian Islands.

Landforms Formed by Crust Movements

Fault: A fault forms when blocks of rock fracture and move.

Mountain: a high, steeply sloped area where rock is uplifted along a fault or created by a volcano.

In this location, the San Andreas Fault created a wide valley, which is filled with water.

Plateau: a high, nearly level, uplifted area composed of horizontal layers of rock. The Colorado River eroded Grand Canyon into the Colorado Plateau.

ES5a. Students know some changes in the earth are due to slow processes, such as erosion, and some changes are due to rapid processes, such as landslides, volcanic eruptions, and earthquakes.

It Happened So Fast!

It takes a few million years to make a rock. Most of the peaks we see today in the Sierra Nevada are more than 2 million years old. The Colorado River began carving Grand Canyon more than 5 million years ago. Most changes to Earth's surface are so slow we can't see them happen.

But sometimes changes happen rapidly. Rapid changes affect people and landforms. Here are some examples of fast changes that have happened in California.

Floods of 1997

Floods caused a lot of damage in northern California in 1997. Three factors created the floods. These were deep snow in the mountains, warm temperatures, and heavy rain.

Yosemite Valley was hit hard. The Merced River rose higher than ever before. Water spread out over much of the valley.

Floodwater in Yosemite

In some places the water was 3 meters (10 feet) deep. Campsites were washed away. Housing for the people who worked in Yosemite was destroyed. When the water slowed, new sand and other sediments were deposited. The course of the river was different. Floodwater has the power to change the land rapidly.

A sign showing the water level during the flood

A Yosemite hiking trail after the flood

Mt. Lassen is a **volcano** in northern California. On May 30, 1914, it became active. Without warning, a blast of steam blew out of its top.

More than 180 steam explosions were recorded over the next year. The explosions blasted a **crater** in Lassen's summit. Finally, on May 19, 1915, hot lava spilled down from the crater.

The crater created by steam blasts in 1914

Lava and mud slides flowing down Mt. Lassen's side

Heat from the eruption melted snow in the area, causing floods and mudflows. Three days later, Lassen let loose a huge blast of hot gases, volcanic ash, and **pumice.** Ash and cinders blew as far as 40 kilometers (25 miles) from the peak. Large areas of northern California were covered with a fresh layer of volcanic ash.

Mt. Lassen was active until 1921. During that time it deposited a lot of new igneous rock over a large area near the volcano. This is an example of mountain building that happened in just a few years.

Lassen is resting again, but for how long? No one can say when, but Lassen will surely erupt again.

A view of the debris after the Mt. Lassen eruption

Northridge Earthquake, 1994

At 4:30 a.m., on January 17, 1994, people living in the Los Angeles area got a jolt. It was an earthquake deep under the city of Northridge, California. The earth shook for 15 seconds.

Earth's crust has a lot of cracks. The cracks are called **faults.** Earthquakes happen when huge blocks of rock slide past each other at a fault.

The Northridge earthquake happened on a fault geologists didn't know about. It was a blind thrust fault. Blind thrust faults don't reach all the way up to Earth's surface. They are hidden faults.

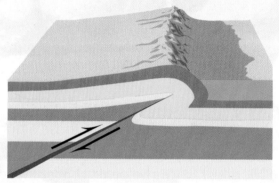

A diagram of a blind thrust fault

Damage was widespread. Sections of major freeways fell. Parking structures and office buildings fell apart. Many apartment buildings were beyond repair. Houses in San Fernando and Santa Monica were also damaged. There were 22,000 people who lost their homes.

Homes and highways damaged in the Northridge quake

San Francisco Earthquake, 1906

Wednesday, April 18, 1906, was the day of the big earthquake in San Francisco. People felt the first little shakes at 5:12 a.m. Soon after, the major shaking started. The shaking lasted 47 seconds. People as far away as southern California, Oregon, and central Nevada felt it.

San Francisco soon after the 1906 earthquake with smoke from fires rising in the background

Movement on the San Andreas Fault caused the 1906 earthquake. The fault broke at Earth's surface for a distance of 470 kilometers (292 miles). Cracks opened and cliffs formed where blocks fell. Land near the San Francisco Bay settled as a result of the shaking. This settling caused buildings to fall over.

Changes to landforms during earthquakes happen faster than during any other common natural event. Earthquakes usually last only a few seconds.

La Conchita Landslides, 1995 and 2005

Landslides occur when rocks and soil slide downhill. Some areas are more likely to have landslides. The hillside above La Conchita, California, is one of those areas. This small town has had two large landslides. The slides killed people and damaged property.

The landslide shown here happened on March 4, 1995. Many people were evacuated because of the slide. Houses nearest the landslide were completely destroyed. No one was killed or injured.

People continued to live in the area below the hillside. Another landslide happened on January 10, 2005. It destroyed or damaged thirty-six houses and killed ten people. This kind of land movement happens so quickly it is often impossible to get out of the way.

The town of La Conchita at the base of an unstable hill

This landslide is another example of erosion and deposition. You can see where the sand and mud eroded from the top of the hill. You can also see where the sediments were deposited on the edge of town.

Yosemite Rockfall, 1996

Ernie Milan was jogging on a trail in Yosemite National Park on July 10, 1996. Ernie was a trail worker for the National Park Service, so he knew the area well. He heard a loud boom! Dust started swirling around him. Day turned into night. What happened?

A giant mass of granite, weighing nearly 70,000 tons, broke loose from a cliff. It fell 600 meters (2,000 feet) to the valley floor. Hundreds of trees were knocked over. One person was killed and several others were injured. Ernie was not hurt.

A 70,000-ton mass of granite fell to the floor of Yosemite Valley.

Scientists estimated that the rock hit the floor at 400 kilometers per hour (250 miles per hour). There is no way to stop rockfalls or predict when they will happen again.

Rockfalls happen all the time in Yosemite. It is a natural kind of weathering and erosion. Most rockfalls are not observed by people. But scientists try to learn what they can from these rockfalls. Some day scientists may be able to predict when a mass of rock is ready to break away.

The broken granite destroyed a large section of forest.

Review Questions

1. What are some ways landforms can change quickly?

2. A volcanic eruption might change Earth's surface in 5 years. Do you think 5 years is a fast change or a slow change? Explain your answer.

3. What effect do landslides have on landforms?

4. What effect do earthquakes have on landforms?

Cynthia Dusel-Bacon: USGS Geologist

Cynthia Dusel-Bacon

ynthia Dusel-Bacon (1946–) is a research geologist with the United States Geological Survey (USGS) in Menlo Park, California. She studies metamorphic rocks in east-central Alaska. During the summer she collects rocks in Alaska. Back in the lab, she uses her microscope to study thin sections of the rocks. She uses all the information she collects to figure out and map the geological history of Alaska.

Collecting rock samples in Alaska

Before Dusel-Bacon became a geologist, she taught Spanish in middle school. When she was studying to get her degree in Spanish, she took a geology course. She loved it! On a field trip near Santa Barbara, California, she found a fossil of a fish. Dusel-Bacon was amazed. Here was a fish that was swimming around in the water millions of years ago. And it is now a fossil in a rock high above the ocean. She was hooked on geology.

When Dusel-Bacon was working as a geology assistant in 1977, something happened that changed her life forever. A helicopter had dropped her off in a remote area of Alaska for the day. While she was collecting rock samples, a black bear came out of the bushes about 3 meters (10 feet) from her. She tried to scare the bear away, but it knocked her to the ground. Dusel-Bacon used her radio to call for help. The helicopter came back and took Dusel-Bacon to the hospital.

Dusel-Bacon lost most of her left arm and all of her right arm. When her injuries healed, she was fitted with artificial arms with hooks. She had to learn new ways to do everything. She did some things, such as writing, eating, and putting on makeup, with her new arms. She learned to use her toes and teeth to do other things.

Turning pages in a book

Dusel-Bacon still does her geology research. She uses equipment that is adapted for her. She uses a tube with a suction cup to place slides on her microscope. She also has foot controls to operate her microscope. She controls her computer with a track ball. It's placed on the floor where she operates it with her foot. And how does she type? Sometimes she uses voice-recognition software so she can talk to her computer. Other times she types with her hook.

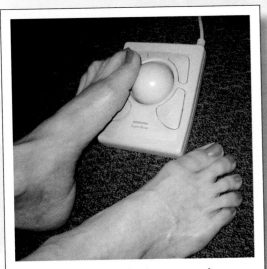
Foot controls for her computer

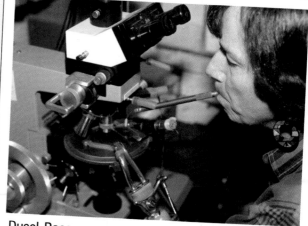
Dusel-Bacon uses a suction cup to place slides on the stage of her microscope.

At home, Dusel-Bacon's husband usually does the cooking. When he's away, Cynthia does all the usual household chores. She uses her feet to cut food with a knife, prepare meals, and wash dishes. She has a special brush in her shower to wash her hair. She drives her car by putting her hook inside a ring on the steering wheel. Dusel-Bacon worked with a babysitter to care for her son, Ian, when he was young. And the whole family has gone to Alaska to do geology fieldwork.

Geology has been a rewarding and interesting career. "As a geologist, I contribute to our understanding of events that shaped the earth millions of years ago. I know there are certain limitations I can't get around, like having to rely on artificial arms. But I certainly am going to do the best I can with all I have. And that's a lot."

Checking location on the way to the study site

Dusel-Bacon, her assistant, and pilot arriving at their study site in Alaska

Dusel-Bacon studies this red mountain to find out what rocks and minerals it is made of.

Summary: Landforms

Earth's surface is solid rock. Rock is hard. It seems like it should last forever. But it doesn't. Rock breaks down. That's weathering.

Many things cause rock to weather. Water expands when it freezes. Water freezing and melting in cracks will break rock into pieces. Tree roots can also break rocks when the roots grow into cracks. When rocks fall, they can break. These are examples of **physical weathering.** Physical weathering makes rocks smaller, but does not change the kind of rock.

When rocks come in contact with acid rain or other chemicals, minerals can change. When minerals change, rocks break down. This is **chemical weathering.** Chemical weathering changes rocks into new materials.

Bits of rock are carried downhill by water. Rocks in streams and rivers bang into one another. They rub against one another. Rocks get smaller and smoother as they move to new locations. The movement of rock materials from one place to another is **erosion.**

Most erosion is caused by flowing water. But wind can also erode rocks. Wind can carry sand and silt to new locations. When the wind stops blowing or the water stops flowing, the eroded rock will settle down. When particles of rock, called sediments, settle down, it is called **deposition.** Sand can be deposited in beaches or sand dunes.

Erosion and deposition can destroy and create **landforms.** Landforms are features of the land, like mountains, canyons, deltas, and beaches. Landforms can also be destroyed and created by other things, such as **earthquakes, landslides,** and **volcanoes.** Volcanoes can create new rock in a short time. In just a few years, a volcano can make a mountain. But it might take 50 million years for the slow processes of weathering and erosion to break down a mountain and carry it to the sea.

Some erosion and deposition can happen fast. Floods, earthquakes, and landslides break and move rock in a few seconds, minutes, or days. Earth's surface is always changing. It is always building up in some places while it is breaking down in other places.

Summary Questions

Now is a good time to review what you have recorded in your science notebook. Think about the investigations you have conducted with rocks and minerals.

1. **Give three examples of weathering.**

2. **What is the difference between chemical and physical weathering?**

3. **Where does the sand on the beach come from?**

4. **Give three examples of deposition.**

5. **How do water and plants weather rocks?**

California Science Standards

ES5a. Students know some changes in the earth are due to slow processes, such as erosion, and some changes are due to rapid processes, such as landslides, volcanic eruptions, and earthquakes.

ES5b. Students know natural processes, including freezing and thawing and the growth of roots, cause rocks to break down into smaller pieces.

ES5c. Students know moving water erodes landforms, reshaping the land by taking it away from some places and depositing it as pebbles, sand, silt, and mud in other places (weathering, transport, and deposition).

Vocabulary

physical weathering

chemical weathering

erosion

deposition

landform

earthquake

landslide

volcano

Learning More about Solid Earth

Rocks and Minerals

Start a Class Rock Collection

Bring rocks to class to share with other students. They can be rocks purchased on vacations or special occasions. Or simply bring in interesting rocks you found in your neighborhood. Make an identification label to go with the rock. Information should include the collector's name, the date of collection, the place it came from, and any additional notes of interest.

Contact the U.S. Geological Survey

The USGS publishes a number of pamphlets and brochures about geology. You can find out about them, and a lot more, at their website. Start with the education link.

Website: http://ask.usgs.gov/index.html

Research Mohs Hardness Scale

Find out more about the hardness scale. Look up the Mohs scale in an encyclopedia or a geology book.

Rock Polishing

Several kinds of rocks and semiprecious minerals, such as agate, amethyst, and rose quartz, are beautiful when polished. The rocks and minerals are placed in a rotating drum with a mixture of abrasive grit and water. After being tumbled for 4–5 weeks, using smaller and smaller grits, the rock surfaces become highly polished. Locate a rock tumbler. Use it to polish some of the rocks from your class rock collection.

Research the California State Mineral and Rock

California has an official state mineral and an official state rock. What are they, and why were they chosen?

Research Rocks Used as Tools

Archaeologists study prehistoric cultures. They often find stone tools that were used for many different jobs. Flint and obsidian have the property of breaking with sharp edges. These rocks were made into sharp tools, such as ax blades, choppers, arrowheads, and daggers. Other kinds of rocks were used for grinding grain. Find out more about how humans used rocks to make tools.

The Fizz Test

Find rocks from as many different locations around the state of California as you can. Test them to see if you can detect calcite in them.

Research Uses of Portland Cement

Find out what portland cement is. Learn where it comes from, when it was invented, who invented it, and what it is used for. Find out what important mineral is in portland cement.

Rocks for Decoration

Early people made pigments from crushed rock. They mixed the colors with animal fat to make paints and dyes. The paints could be used to decorate homes, pottery, or skin.

People have always used rocks and minerals to create decorative jewelry. Research the use of rocks and minerals for decoration in ancient times and in the present day.

Rock Art

The art of Japanese stone arranging is called bon-seki. It is believed that the beauty of rocks rests not only in the rocks themselves, but in their relationships. Bring in rocks or use the class rock collection to practice bon-seki.

Landforms

Take Stream-Table Photos

Take video or digital still images of the stream tables in action. Make the images into a report to share with the class.

Plan a Field Trip

Take a field trip in your local area. You might visit a nature center on a river, an Army Corps of Engineers project such as a dam and reservoir site or stream model, or the water utilities offices.

Find a Local Erosion-Control Expert

Find out which agencies are responsible for erosion control in your area. Look into the Soil Conservation Service, Flood Control, and so forth. Invite a guest speaker to describe the work the agency performs and the specific problems the group is working on.

Go on a 15-Minute Field Trip

Go on a schoolyard field trip right after a hard rain. What evidence of erosion and deposition can you find? Look for places where sand and soil have been deposited. How are these places similar to what you saw in the stream tables?

Describe Stream-Table Landforms

Pretend you are a tiny traveler walking around in your stream table. Describe the landforms and other sights that you see. Use the landform vocabulary words.

How Much Is a Million?

Geologists think that it took 5–6 million years for the Colorado River to erode Grand Canyon. How big is 1,000,000? Figure out how long it takes to live 1,000,000 seconds. Come up with some comparisons and estimates of your own. For example, how many grains of rice are there in a 1-liter container?

Write a Stream Haiku

Haiku is unrhymed Japanese poetry made up of three lines. The first line has five syllables, the second line has seven, and the last line has five. Here is an example.

Creek

Water flowing clear;

Bubbling, dancing, leaping by;

Where does water go?

Try writing your own haiku about a stream.

Research Big Rivers

Find out about big rivers around the world. Where are their headwaters and mouths? What countries do they flow through? How long are they? What are the largest rivers in the United States? What are the largest rivers in California?

Earth Sciences Glossary

Abrasion   The rubbing, grinding, and bumping of rocks that cause physical weathering.

Acid   A substance that geologists use to identify rocks that contain calcite.

Bauxite   An ore for the metal aluminum.

Birthstone   A gem mineral that is identified with a month of the year.

Calcite   A common rock-forming mineral in Earth's crust.

Carbonate   A mineral that contains carbon and oxygen.

Chalk   A form of calcium carbonate.

Chemical reaction   A process in which chemical substances change into new substances.

Chemical weathering   The process by which the minerals in a rock can change due to chemicals in water and air. Chemical weathering can change rocks and cause them to break apart.

Cleavage   The appearance of the surfaces of freshly broken minerals.

Core   The center of Earth, which is made mostly of iron and nickel.

Crater   A hole or depression.

Crust   Earth's hard outer layer of solid rock.

Crystal   A natural form of a mineral. Crystal shape can help to identify a mineral.

Deposition   The settling of sediments.

Dissolve   When one material disappears in another material.

Earthquake   A sudden movement of Earth's crust along a fault.

Erosion   The carrying away of weathered earth materials by water, wind, or ice.

Evaporate   To dry up.

Evidence   Observations that help a person to form a conclusion.

Expose   To leave in the open with no protection.

Fault   A break in Earth's crust along which blocks of rock move past each other.

Feldspar   A common rock-forming mineral in Earth's crust.

Flood   Covered with water.

Fossil   Any remains, trace, or imprint of animal or plant life preserved in Earth's crust.

Fracture   The uneven, rounded, or splintered surfaces of some minerals when they break.

Gem   A hard mineral that can be cut into beautiful shapes.

Geologist   A scientist who studies Earth, its materials, and its history.

Glacier   A large mass of slow-moving ice.

Gold   A valuable metal that is found in gold ore.

Granite   An igneous rock that forms underground.

Hardness   A property of minerals determined by trying to scratch them with different materials.

Hematite   An ore mineral containing the metal iron.

Igneous rock   Any rock that forms when melted rock (magma) hardens.

Landform   A feature of the land, such as a mountain, canyon, or beach.

Landslide   The movement of earth materials down a slope.

Lava   Melted rock erupting onto Earth's surface, usually from a volcano.

Limestone   A sedimentary rock made mostly of calcite.

Luster   A description of the way light reflects off the surface of a freshly broken mineral.

Magma   Melted rock below Earth's surface.

Magnetic   A property of minerals that are attracted to magnets.

Malachite   An ore mineral containing the metal copper.

Mantle   The solid rock material between Earth's core and crust.

Marble   A metamorphic rock formed when limestone is subjected to heat and pressure.

Metallic   A description of the luster of a mineral that shines like metal.

Metamorphic rock   A kind of rock that forms when rocks and minerals are subjected to heat, pressure, or both.

Microscope   An instrument that makes small objects appear larger.

Mineral   An ingredient in a rock.

Mock rock   A fake or imitation rock.

Nonmetallic   A description of the luster of a mineral that does not shine like a metal.

Opaque   Any matter that does not let light shine through it.

Ore   A rock or mineral that has a valuable substance in it, such as gold.

Ore mineral   A mineral from which a valuable material, usually a metal, is extracted.

Outcrop   A mass of rock exposed at Earth's surface.

Physical weathering   The process by which rocks are broken down by breaking and banging.

Property   A characteristic that describes an object, such as size, shape, and texture.

Pumice   A type of rock that forms when lava erupts from volcanoes.

Quartz   A common metamorphic rock.

React   To act or change in response to something.

Rock   A solid earth material usually made of two or more minerals.

Rock cycle   The processes by which rocks change into different kinds of rocks.

Rock-forming mineral   A mineral that combines with other minerals to form rocks.

Sandstone   A sedimentary rock made of sand particles cemented together.

Sediment   Pieces of weathered rock such as sand, deposited by wind, water, and ice.

Sedimentary rock   A rock that forms in layers when sediments get cemented together.

Smelting   The process of melting metal ores in order to separate the pure metal.

Stalactite   A rock formation containing calcite that hangs from the ceilings of caves.

Streak   The line left behind when a mineral sample is rubbed on a tile.

Thin section   A rock sample that is thin enough for light to shine through.

Transparent   Anything that is clear and lets light shine through it.

Transport   To move or carry from one place to another.

Travertine   A rock containing calcite, often found around hot springs.

Tufa   A rock containing calcite, often found in stalactites.

Volcano   An opening in Earth's crust where lava, cinders, ash, and gases come to the surface.

Wave A moving mass of water created by wind or tides.

Weathering The process by which larger rocks are cracked and broken over time to form smaller rocks.

References

Table of Contents

References

Science Safety Rules

1. Listen carefully to your teacher's instructions. Follow all directions. Ask questions if you don't know what to do.

2. Tell your teacher if you have any allergies.

3. Never put any materials in your mouth. Do not taste anything unless your teacher tells you to do so.

4. Never smell any unknown material. If your teacher tells you to smell something, wave your hand over the material to bring the smell toward your nose.

5. Do not touch your face, mouth, ears, eyes, or nose while working with chemicals, plants, or animals.

6. Always protect your eyes. Wear safety goggles when necessary. Tell your teacher if you wear contact lenses.

7. Always wash your hands with soap and warm water after handling chemicals, plants, or animals.

8. Never mix any chemicals unless your teacher tells you to do so.

9. Report all spills, accidents, and injuries to your teacher.

10. Treat animals with respect, caution, and consideration.

11. Clean up your work space after each investigation.

12. Act responsibly during all science activities.

CA FOSSweb

Go to www.FOSSweb.com/CA to find activities for each FOSS module. You will also find interesting books to read, vocabulary lists, and links to related websites. This site was designed for you to use with friends and family at home. For your parents, there is information about each FOSS module and copies of the Home/School Connections.

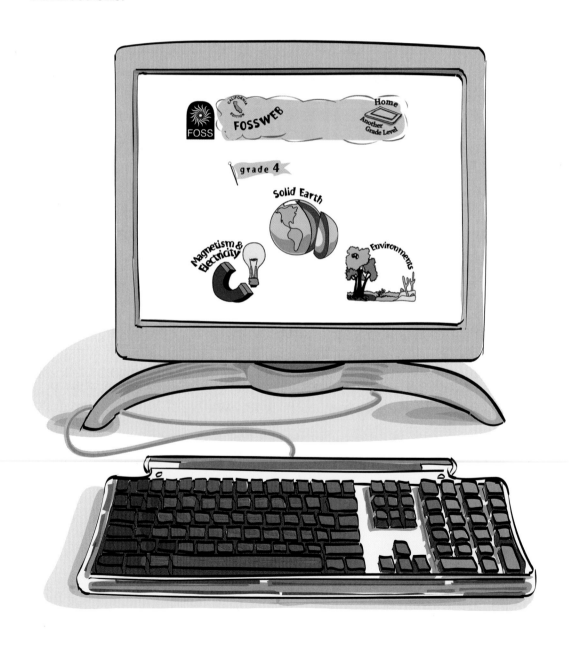

California Science Content Standards for Grade 4

Physical Sciences

1. Electricity and magnetism are related effects that have many useful applications in everyday life. As a basis for understanding this concept:

   a. *Students know* how to design and build simple series and parallel circuits by using components, such as wires, batteries, and bulbs.

   b. *Students know* how to build a simple compass and use it to detect magnetic effects, including Earth's magnetic field.

   c. *Students know* electric currents produce magnetic fields and know how to build a simple electromagnet.

   d. *Students know* the role of electromagnets in the construction of electric motors, electric generators, and simple devices, such as doorbells, and earphones.

   e. *Students know* electrically charged objects attract or repel each other.

   f. *Students know* that magnets have two poles (north and south) and that like poles repel each other while unlike poles attract each other.

   g. *Students know* electrical energy can be converted to heat, light, and motion.

Life Sciences

2. All organisms need energy and matter to live and grow. As a basis for understanding this concept:

    a. *Students know* plants are the primary source of matter and energy entering most food chains.

    b. *Students know* producers and consumers (herbivores, carnivores, omnivores, and decomposers) are related in food chains and food webs and may compete with each other for resources in an ecosystem.

    c. *Students know* decomposers, including many fungi, insects, and microorganisms, recycle matter from dead plants and animals.

3. Living organisms depend on one another and on their environment for survival. As a basis for understanding this concept:

    a. *Students know* ecosystems can be characterized by their living and nonliving components.

    b. *Students know* that in any particular environment, some kinds of plants and animals survive well, some survive less well, and some cannot survive at all.

    c. *Students know* many plants depend on animals for pollination and seed dispersal, and animals depend on plants for food and shelter.

    d. *Students know* that most microorganisms do not cause disease and that many are beneficial.

Earth Sciences

4. The properties of rocks and minerals reflect the processes that formed them. As a basis for understanding this concept:

    a. *Students know* how to differentiate among igneous, sedimentary, and metamorphic rocks by referring to their properties and methods of formation (the rock cycle).

    b. *Students know* how to identify common rock-forming minerals (including quartz, calcite, feldspar, mica, and hornblende) and ore minerals by using a table of diagnostic properties.

5. Waves, wind, water, and ice shape and reshape Earth's land surface. As a basis for understanding this concept:

   a. *Students know* some changes in the earth are due to slow processes, such as erosion, and some changes are due to rapid processes, such as landslides, volcanic eruptions, and earthquakes.

   b. *Students know* natural processes, including freezing and thawing and the growth of roots, cause rocks to break down into smaller pieces.

   c. *Students know* moving water erodes landforms, reshaping the land by taking it away from some places and depositing it as pebbles, sand, silt, and mud in other places (weathering, transport, and deposition).

Investigation and Experimentation

6. Scientific progress is made by asking meaningful questions and conducting careful investigations. As a basis for understanding this concept and addressing the content in the other three strands, students should develop their own questions and perform investigations. Students will:

   a. Differentiate observation from inference (interpretation) and know scientists' explanations come partly from what they observe and partly from how they interpret their observations.

   b. Measure and estimate the weight, length, or volume of objects.

   c. Formulate and justify predictions based on cause-and-effect relationships.

   d. Conduct multiple trials to test a prediction and draw conclusions about the relationships between predictions and results.

   e. Construct and interpret graphs from measurements.

   f. Follow a set of written instructions for a scientific investigation.

Photo Credits

About the Cover: A California gull

Index